MW01096451

"Denis Sheeran has done ⌐⌐⌐⌐⌐⌐⌐ ⌐uoyant and breezy style of writing, he ⌐as written a critically timely book to help all math teachers navigate the complex world of digital kids, social media, and emergent pedagogy. Written with the acute and authoritative framework of a 'white paper', but with the signature humor and empathy of Sheeran, *Hacking Mathematics* is easily one of the most accessible and desirable reads that I have come across in the crowded field of math education books! Each chapter has the same effective flow of ideas—The Problem, The Hack, What You Can Do Tomorrow, Full Implementation, and Pushback. Chapters offer solutions to problems that range from the micro (solving the calculator dilemma) to the macro (creating a culture of inquiry). Sheeran, with his vast experience as a classroom teacher, musician, and sports coach, has woven his charming prose with today's cultural references to create a book that will be an instant game-changer in every math classroom! At the vacant intersection of Practicality and Personality is where you will find the long-awaited *Hacking Mathematics!*"

SUNIL SINGH
AUTHOR OF PI OF LIFE: THE HIDDEN HAPPINESS OF MATHEMATICS

"Denis Sheeran captures ten easy changes that any math teacher at any grade level can apply in their classrooms tomorrow to make their lessons more engaging and relevant. Busy teachers will appreciate the fact that he not only highlights changes that should be made but gives step-by-step directions for implementing each change. This book will make any teacher think critically about how their day-to-day classroom decisions can create an environment where students value and explore mathematics.

As math teachers, we naturally ask our students a lot of questions. But, are we asking our students the right questions? Denis Sheeran tackles this question and many other easy-to-implement changes that math teachers can make tomorrow to increase student engagement in their classrooms."

SARAH CARTER
HIGH SCHOOL MATH TEACHER AND AUTHOR OF MATH = LOVE BLOG

"It has taken my entire career to learn how I might teach my math lessons more effectively than the way I was taught in school. Denis Sheeran has successfully created a shortcut that will transform your teaching and save you years of experimenting. Denis Sheeran has managed to create a shortcut to solving some of the biggest problems we encounter daily, so you can start making changes in a matter of hours instead of years.

Dive into this easy to read book full of hacks that solve some of the biggest problems math teachers face in their classrooms. Denis Sheeran takes on the problems created through using many of the traditional math lesson routines and provides the reader with easy to implement strategies that not only eliminate the problem, but also promote deeper student understanding.

From hacks to address problems around homework, warm-up routines and math practice to making math relevant to keep students engaged in learning and loving math, it is clear that Sheeran has very carefully selected 10 problems that are worth solving in your math classroom. This is a book I would gladly give any teacher in my district to help them think differently about how we can most effectively deliver our math curriculum."

KYLE PEARCE
K-12 MATHEMATICS CONSULTANT
GREATER ESSEX COUNTY DISTRICT SCHOOL BOARD
WINDSOR, ONTARIO, CANADA

"A must read for all teachers of mathematics. It's time to take an honest look at traditional math teaching, get real about that which doesn't work, and innovate around ways to 'hack' our instruction in order to engage students in creative problem solving and innovation that will improve learning and improve lives."

AMY FAST
HIGH SCHOOL ASSISTANT PRINCIPAL AND AUTHOR OF *IT'S THE MISSION, NOT THE MANDATES*

"Denis Sheeran does it again! In this text, he brings his expertise and passion for the study of mathematics in order to provide practical and pedagogical support to the everyday teacher. As educators, it is imperative to do something to help diminish the fear of math that encompasses many educators and students. Sheeran has thought of every problem in the book (no pun intended) that can stop a teacher from making math more approachable. Every chapter concludes with simple solutions that can be immediately implemented. This honest and humorous book can not only by enjoyed by everyday teachers, but also by educational leaders who want to enhance their pedagogical practice."

SYLWIA DENKO
3RD GRADE TEACHER AND TECHNOLOGY COACH

"Denis Sheeran delivers again with *Hacking Mathematics*. It is the perfect guide for making math come alive in the classroom with practical ideas for bringing the world into the classroom, shifting that dreaded homework review into an active practice time, and so, so much more. This book offers 10 useful math hacks that all teachers of math will be able to implement into their classrooms tomorrow."

MARGIE PEARSE
MATH CONSULTANT AND CO-AUTHOR OF *TEACHING NUMERACY,
LEARNING THAT NEVER ENDS* AND *PASSING THE MATHEMATICS TEST FOR
ELEMENTARY TEACHERS*

"In the sea of mathematics education books available, *Hacking Mathematics: 10 Problems That Need Solving* is THE book that all current and prospective math teachers need to read. In this book, Denis Sheeran offers a new perspective on what it means to be a math teacher and to teach math. The 10 highly relatable 'Hacks' outlined in the text offer philosophy, best-practices, and examples, along with what you can implement into your classroom the very next day. Although every Hack might not apply to every math teacher and classroom, all math teachers are guaranteed to come away with easy to implement, practical, yet incredibly powerful strategies that are sure to impact their learners in the most positive of ways.

Many students often question why they need to learn many of the things in math that are taught in schools. No student in your classroom will be left feeling this way and will carry with them the concepts learned, beyond just passing a test. The experiences you will be able to provide for your students after reading this book will ensure that their learning will be authentic and will endure.

This book is truly a fantastic resource for those who want to embrace the full potential of what it means to be a math educator."

LAURA FLEMING
LIBRARY MEDIA SPECIALIST, AUTHOR OF *WORLDS OF MAKING: BEST PRACTICES FOR ESTABLISHING A MAKERSPACE FOR YOUR SCHOOL* AND *THE KICKSTART GUIDE TO MAKING GREAT MAKERSPACES*

"Math instruction is in crisis. So many students struggle to connect what they're learning with the real world—one that demands solid math skills in many highly sought-after careers. Denis Sheeran provides a toolbox for math teachers who want something different—something BETTER—than page 190 1-20 odds."

MATT MILLER
TEACHER, AUTHOR OF *DITCH THAT TEXTBOOK*

"*Hacking Mathematics* is a great resource for any teacher! Every hack is easily laid out for helping you transform your classroom. Denis Sheeran provides the reader with what they can implement tomorrow, a blueprint for full implementation, tips to overcoming pushback, and what the Hack looks like in action. *Hacking Mathematics* is easy to read and a great tool for creating a meaningful experience in your classroom.

Are you looking for ways to make your class more engaging? Do you want to implement change and build your learning community, but you aren't quite where to begin? *Hacking Mathematics* provides applicable resources to engage students in mathematics. Sheeran discusses homework, blogging, Twitter, MTBOS, Desmos, and more!"

JULIA FINNEYFROCK
UPPER SCHOOL MATH TEACHER

"*Hacking Mathematics* is a user-friendly guide to support the transformation of mathematics instruction through relevance and connections to our world. Denis clearly defines the importance of shifting our mindsets from how we learned mathematics, to empowering kids with a mathematical mindset. Every teacher of math will benefit from this book, and their students will as well."

BETHANY HILL
ELEMENTARY PRINCIPAL

"In his new book, math educator Denis Sheeran shares a handful of hacks to energize math instruction in your classroom. With teacher stories, recommendations for tools, and descriptions of strategies he's used with students, Sheeran provides actionable information for math educators."

MONICA BURNS
AUTHOR OF *TASKS BEFORE APPS* AND FOUNDER OF CLASSTECHTIPS.COM

HACKING
MATHEMATICS

HACKING
MATHEMATICS
10 Problems That Need Solving

Denis Sheeran

x10
PUBLICATIONS

Hacking Mathematics
© 2018 by Times 10 Publications

These books are available at special discounts when purchased in quantity for use as premiums, promotions, fundraising, and educational use. For inquiries and details, contact us at www.hacklearning.org.

Published by Times 10
Highland Heights, OH
Times10Books.com

Project Management by Kelly Schuknecht
Cover Design by Najdan Mancic
Interior Design by Steven Plummer
Editing by Jennifer Jas
Proofreading by Carrie White-Parrish

Library of Congress Cataloging-in-Publication Data is available.
ISBN: 978-1-948212-03-8
First Printing: March, 2018

CONTENTS

Introduction 13
The biggest problem of them all

Hack 1: Help Them See Math Everywhere 19
Engaging all students from the start of class

Hack 2: Pull a Double Switch and Add Practice Time . . 35
Applying best practices for practicing best

Hack 3: Join the MTBoS 49
Bringing the global math teaching community into your classroom

Hack 4: Encourage a Digital Show and Tell 59
Using a 1:1 environment to demonstrate understanding

Hack 5: Be Less Helpful and Ask More Questions 69
Turning mathematical struggles into deep learning

Hack 6: Go Prospecting for Relevant Learning 79
Making mathematics real and increasing student engagement

Hack 7: Solve the Calculator Conundrum 93
Choosing an instrument for all students: Desmos

Hack 8: Ask Unanswerable Questions 107
Engaging students in statistical thinking instead of skipping that section

Hack 9: Create a Wonderwall 119
Building a culture of inquiry

Hack 10: Communicate the Message with Two-by-Fours 129
Creating community and parent buy-in

Conclusion 141
Putting the pieces together

Other Books in the *Hack Learning Series* 143
Hack Learning Resources 159
About the Author 161

INTRODUCTION

The biggest problem of them all

I BEGAN TEACHING HIGH school mathematics in January of 1999. I was fresh out of college, excited to teach, and ready to give it my all every day. Much of that excitement and energy stuck with me for the next thirteen years as I taught math at Lake Forest High School in Lake Forest, Illinois. I was lucky to be surrounded by passionate, dedicated math teachers who were interested both in doing the best job that they could, and in finding ways to help their students achieve their potential and beyond in mathematics. This environment, it turns out, is not mirrored in every math department across the country. It was when I became an administrator, supervising math teachers and observing their practices and daily activities, that I became aware of a sobering fact: There are math teachers who don't actually like math. This, in my opinion, is the biggest problem of them all.

Math has a bad rap already. There are countless adults out there who, when you tell them you're a math teacher, will take out a cross and garlic and pray for the sun to come out, just to get your mathematical vampire ways out of their sight. "I'm not a math person and was never any good at math" might as well be an option for people to choose on personality profiles or dating sites. When people tell you to "do the math," it usually ends up with a less-than-desirable result. And ask any parents of school-age children, when they ask them if they have any home-work that night, how their sons or daughters say the phrase "math homework." I can guarantee you that it's not with glee and delight. At least that's not how the older two of my four children say it.

So it's disheartening to know that there are TEACHERS of math out there—in schools, right now—who don't like the subject about which they themselves are charged with communicating value to students. These are the same students who'll become adults, and one day will ask a person what she does for a living, and will have to respond when that person says, "I'm a math teacher."

But, as you'll read throughout this book, you'll see that I'm a hopeful person. I believe that teachers of math who don't like math can once again become lovers of math.

I believe that the math those people don't like isn't the math that they should be teaching, but outdated mathematical skill sets and thoughtless approaches to replicating mathematical steps.

In this book, I've brought attention to ten issues with mathematics teaching and learning today. Some of the Hacks I demonstrate for solving these problems are new ways of approaching teaching. Others are new ways for students to communicate their learning. Some involve technology and others do not. Each Hack may resonate with a practice you use in your classroom now or a challenge you've been facing as an educator in recent months and years, or it may be new to you but visible in the classroom next door. It's my hope that these Hacks will lead to valuable change in your classroom and in the experiences your students have while learning mathematics.

Who will benefit the most from reading this book? If you are at all involved in the teaching of mathematics, then you are the intended audience of this book. If you're a math teacher, a pre-service teacher looking for your first job, a teacher returning to the profession after years away, or a supervisor or administrator who observes math teachers, then the strategies inside *Hacking Mathematics* can provide the framework for moving mathematics teaching forward in your school.

Does that mean that every Hack in the book will work for every teacher? Of course it does. Apply every one of them to every one of your classes every day, starting now!

Or, if you're a rational adult, apply these new strategies to your classroom with an open mind, as they best fit into your teaching. Let someone else in your school know that you're making changes, so they can provide objective, meaningful feedback in a non-confrontational and evaluative way. This will also promote the culture of change that I believe you truly want in your school, which is why you're reading this book. If you prefer the status quo, however, check out most Algebra 1 textbooks, or classrooms that require students to do math only in pencil. You'll find it there.

Some of these Hacks come from my own experiences in the classroom or as an administrator observing math classes. Others come from excellent math teachers, across the country, who I've had the pleasure and luck to work and collaborate with over the past couple years. You may have already heard about some of the strategies in this book, or may even be using them now. That's great. The more people who have a mindset for improving mathematics instruction in this world, the better. I encourage you to share your versions of these Hacks with me and the educational community. Where can you do that? By Hack 3, you'll know exactly how.

I hope that one or more of these Hacks stands out to you. I hope that the ideas that begin to grow in your mind as a result of reading this book blossom into effective practices that re-invigorate your passion for teaching mathematics and for creating a generation of students who love learning math. When the famous author G.K. Chesterton was asked, "What's wrong with the world today?" by *The Times*, he famously wrote and mailed back this succinct response:

> Dear Sir,
> I am.
> Yours,
> G.K. Chesterton

What's wrong with math teaching today? Is it technology? Is it "the clientele?" Is it leadership and micromanagement? Or is it something else?

Let's solve some math problems.

HELP THEM SEE MATH EVERYWHERE

Engaging all students from the start of class

Think before you act.
— Mom

THE PROBLEM: THE "DO NOW" DOESN'T DO IT ANYMORE

FIRST IMPRESSIONS. DAILY first impressions. Each and every day, math teachers have the chance to make a new first impression on students. And each and every day, teachers blow it with a Do Now problem. It's there in the lesson plan template provided by district leadership and it's an expected part of the daily class routine … the anticipatory set. There's a good chance that each day as you prepare for class, you do what you were taught to do for this part of the lesson. You pick one of the homework problems that you assigned (odds, so they can check their answers but never do?) and put it up on the board for students to work on while you take attendance, check for homework completion (see Hack 2), and then ask, "Does anyone have any questions about the Do Now?" If they do, then you go over it. After one hundred eighty or so of these, you're on summer vacation.

A handful of your students did the homework assignment completely and got all of the answers correct: Your Do Now is failing them. Other students didn't do any of the homework, so they don't really know if they have any questions for you: Your Do Now is failing them, too. Still other students have genuine questions for you and will be confused by the Do Now, which is also failing them.

Perhaps you've put up these other Do Now activities at the start of class:

- A problem similar to, but not one of the homework problems

- A problem from today's lesson, to get them looking forward

- A problem from a previous lesson that's going to be on an upcoming assessment

- A problem the students asked you to do from the homework

So, each class begins with a problem—a problem that needs solving. The start of each class should be much more than an attempt to continue a learning conversation from the previous day. The traditional Do Now problem is just that: an attempt to connect yesterday to today, to bring the students back into the conversation. The issues lie in the number of conversations that your students have had since you closed yours out the day before, and in understanding that they're all coming from different conversations before they come to yours. Your students are coming from science, social studies, English, world language, gym (middle school odors included), music, home (where there may or may not have been breakfast ... or peace), or a number of other places. They're all coming into your classroom to learn math. Is your Do Now problem effective at putting them all on the same track and bringing them all into the same conversation with you? My guess is, probably not. It didn't work when I tried it, so I tried something else.

> **Our students need to be prepared to engage in the type of thinking and analysis that we want them to do during our time in class. It is time to move from Do Now to Think Now.**

All my life I've been a musician. I have been playing saxophone since fourth grade, singing since I had a voice, and I play a mean slide whistle (I would have totally had a career as a Foley artist if this math thing hadn't taken off). As a sax player, I warm up before I perform or practice.

If I'm working on a song involving lots of fast running notes, it doesn't make sense for me to warm up with long, smooth tones. It's the same thing if I'm going to play a slow, lyrical piece. I shouldn't warm up with flexibility and speed exercises. Those don't get me ready to do the job I'm about to do.

I also enjoyed being a track and field coach for much of my teaching career. At first, I coached the distance runners: those who ran races of eight hundred meters or more. I had them go for an easy jog warmup, then sit and stretch before running a distance workout on the track. When I became the head coach, I took over coaching the sprinters, relay teams, and hurdlers. Does it make sense for me to send them on the same warmup as the distance runners? Not at all. These athletes were about to perform in an entirely different way than the distance runners. If I had them go for a jog, then sit down to stretch, the first few minutes of running a sprinter's workout would destroy them as athletes. Neither their bodies nor their central nervous systems would have been prepared to do the activity that I wanted them to do. Each group of athletes needed a different type of warmup to be able to perform at their best.

I feel the same way about beginning a math class. Our students need to be prepared to engage in the type of thinking and analysis that we want them to do during our time in class. It is time to move from Do Now to Think Now.

THE HACK: HELP THEM SEE MATH EVERYWHERE

Pull back the Do Now question that is directly related to the homework or the lesson and think for a minute about the TYPE of activity your students will need to do during their time in your classroom. If they're just going to sit and listen to you talk for forty-five minutes to an hour, then this chapter doesn't pertain to you. Those students won't actually be doing anything. If, however, you intend for your students to engage in mathematical problem-solving, communicating their solutions or ideas, and collaborating with each other during the process, then this Hack is for you.

The Hack is simple. In Google Slides or PowerPoint, whichever your school subscribes to, create an "I See Math" starter to kick off the class. Keep it simple with white backgrounds and no fancy stuff. Here's what to include on the slides:

> Slide 1: A title
>
> Slide 2: A picture of something you saw that has a potential to raise questions for your students or spark curiosity, even if the questions may not be truly answerable
>
> Slide 3: A vague question to get them going

Here's an example. I titled it "Too Much Coffee" then showed the students this picture for about thirty seconds:

On the third slide, I posed this question: *I love coffee. My wife says that if I ever die, they may actually find some blood in my caffeine stream. I'm interested in getting the most bang for my caffeinated buck. What should I buy?*

This question had my "mathy" students instantly jumping to finding the unit rate or the price per ounce. The fun part is that they didn't come to a conflict until their last calculation. It was at that point that they had their "mind blown" moment. Why would I ask them a question that didn't have a simple answer that could be found out by a set of calculations? I asked them this question because it would give all of the students an opportunity to engage with it based on how they viewed the problem, not how quickly they could do a calculation.

A few students began to ask about the ratios of ice and coffee compared to hot coffees. Others asked about the size of the cups and wondered if a twenty-four-ounce iced coffee was twenty-four ounces of coffee, plus ice, or less coffee plus ice, totaling twenty-four ounces. At least one student decided that I should buy the large iced coffee because it said "Most Refreshing Value" below it. Still other students even began to dive into the idea that the caffeine level was what was most important and that we should investigate further how much caffeine was in iced coffee versus hot coffee.

You see, what students were doing during this brief period was looking at a situation, identifying what parts were important to them, ignoring the parts that were not important to them, performing calculations, sharing those ideas with others next to them, trying to communicate those ideas clearly to convince their neighbors that they were right, and revising their thoughts based on the input of others. In my opinion, those are the major facets of an effective math classroom. If I can ask my students a question that engages them in that way every day, then whether I'm about to talk about parabolas or the volumes of three-dimensional solids, their mindsets are focused on the situations I'm about to present to them, how to approach those situations, and what to do as they engage in the questions I ask. Virtually no Do Now question I ever asked brought all of my students into the conversation so effectively and so immediately.

WHAT YOU CAN DO TOMORROW

You have, at your fingertips, the opportunity to bring the world into your classroom. If you're a modern adult, you likely have a smartphone nearby as you read this. Put it to work as an effective collection tool and start bringing aspects of your world into your classroom.

- **Check your phone for interesting mathematical pictures right now.** Look for images with patterns, geometric shapes, intersecting lines, arrays, and more. I'm sure you have a few good ones that can spark questions.

- **Create an I See Math slides file.** Follow the simple three-slide format above. Take note: Don't ask your students a concrete question. Keep it vague, but necessary.

- **Start your next class with an I See Math.** When you open class, instead of using the Do Now, tell the story of how you took the picture that led to your question. Bring your students into the story and see what directions their wonderings go.

- **Evaluate your classroom culture.** Pay attention to your students as they engage in this. Resist the urge to jump in and help them or

lead them to the end too quickly. Remember,
you're warming them up for your class, and
you need the warmup to last.

- **Start taking lots of pictures.** The more you
see math all around you, the more you can
bring I See Math to your students.

A BLUEPRINT FOR FULL IMPLEMENTATION

Step 1: Inform your supervisors that you're changing the nature of your anticipatory set.

Despite my idealistic view of education in general, I realize
that some administrators just like things the way they like
them. If you've been required to list a Do Now question as
a component of your lesson planning, you'll need to have
a conversation with your supervisor or administrator. Let
them know that you are trying a new idea, explain why,
and tell them you will monitor the effectiveness of this procedure as you try it out.

Having an open conversation with your supervisor is
not always easy. In some schools there's a negative relationship between teachers and administration, and I've
been on both sides of that situation. I've found that when
we discuss an idea that would benefit the students, any
negativity and animosity fall to the wayside, and both
sides usually become more open. If you are currently

working in a school environment that invites innovation, curiosity, and new teaching techniques, then you may be able to skip this step altogether and jump right to Step 2.

Step 2: Choose how often you'd like to add I See Math.

Use it as often as possible; realistically, you may want to try it once per chapter or unit until you become comfortable managing the classroom environment and effectively organizing an exit from this question into your lesson. You can move from once per chapter into once a week, or if you find yourself with enough questions from photos, you may want to go with it daily. I found that students do not tire quickly of the questions because each is so unique and inherently interesting. Students often start up a side conversation that centers around where I was at the time I took the picture. So not only are they trying to answer the vague mathematical question about the image, but they're also trying to figure out an answer to a question I didn't ask. That holds almost as much value in the process as the question itself.

Step 3: Create a library of I See Math questions.

Once you're in the I See Math mindset, you will see things to photograph and add to your collection. I have taken pictures of item prices, artworks, buildings, sunsets, animals, patterns on furniture, and virtually anything else that catches my eye. Often, I don't have a question associated with that photo right away, but I come up with one later. For the times that you do have a question stirring as you see the image, I encourage you to install Google Slides on your phone. I created a three-slide template and saved it as a shortcut on my phone's home screen. When I see an image that I plan to share as an I See Math question, I open up the template, take the picture directly onto the second slide, and quickly add a title to the first slide and the question to the third. Voila! I've now got the entire file ready to present in class. Google Slides is easy to use from your phone, and if you're in Google Classroom, you can share it directly to your classroom stream if you'd like students to think about that question anytime, not just at the start of class.

One of the most interesting things that came out of this process was that my students began to take their own pictures of things that were mathematically interesting. All of a sudden, I didn't need to be the one coming up with all of the pictures and ideas for class. Bringing students into this process not only gives them ownership over their learning, but if you're using the Danielson Framework for your evaluations, this goes deep into the distinguished category as students take an active role in the activities planned for your classroom.

Step 4: Share the idea with other math teachers to build support.

If you find that I See Math is generating curiosity, thoughtful approaches to problem-solving, and exciting mathematical discourse, then don't keep it to yourself. Share the idea with other teachers and see if they are willing to try it out as well. If students in your school are consistently receiving opportunities to engage in mathematical thinking, even when in different classrooms, the similar experiences will mean smoother transitions when they change classes the next year. An added benefit of sharing this idea with other teachers and developing a supportive partnership between colleagues is that if your administration has a negative view of innovative teaching and change, you can overcome that view when you're not the only one using a strategy.

Step 5: Invite teachers or administrators into your room to see I See Math in action.

Openness, honesty, and transparency are key in your classroom practices. (And by transparency, I don't mean the see-through film and Vis-A-Vis markers you taught with in the '90s, but here's a bonus Hack: Keep the film and markers and use them on desktops as see-through dry-erase boards.) If you invite other teachers into your classroom to see this Hack in action, they may want to introduce it into their own classrooms. They'll also be able to give you objective feedback on what they saw the students doing while they were engaging with the question. This can help you revise and refine your procedures, and become aware of student thinking you may have missed. Inviting the administration into your classroom says to them that you have nothing to hide, that you are interested in making your learning environment engaging, fun, and effective, and that you value their opinions. That gesture goes a long way and may build a level of support for you the next time you try an innovative idea.

OVERCOMING PUSHBACK

Long-standing habits, expectations, and comfort zones often make it difficult to change an established procedure. Here are a few comments you might get from other teachers, and how to address them.

My students need to do a practice problem at the start of class. This is a teacher's habit, not a student's need. If teachers say this to you, they should be the first you invite into your classroom to see I See Math in action. Not confrontationally, of course, but ask them, as respected colleagues, for their opinions on this new activity you're trying out with your students.

I'll score lower on my evaluation if my supervisor doesn't see the Do Now. Great. Call the I See Math problem the Do Now on your lesson plan. Label it Do Now on the slides presentation. By all means, it's the Do Now, only it's not about doing, it's about thinking. If anyone asks, your Do Now (I See Math) was brief, got their attention, activated prior learning, and prepared them for the day's learning. That's the definition of an anticipatory set.

The kids don't seem interested. Start using their pictures sooner. If students begin to see their classmates' pictures becoming part of the lesson, the natural follow-up is to bring in their own. If you know anything about the lives of your students, such as where they work or hang out, then you can suggest mathematically interesting ideas for their pictures. Once they begin to see the possibilities, their natural curiosity and competitive nature will drive them to take more pictures, and more unique pictures, to share in class.

THE HACK IN ACTION

I introduced this hack at Twitter Math Camp 2016 (#TMC16) at Augsburg College in Minneapolis, Minnesota. Yes, Twitter Math Camp is a real thing: Google it, then go to it. It's awesome. Since then, teachers have included the hashtag #ISeeMath when sharing images that spark curiosity. Check it out on Twitter for an instant library of images and questions to bring into your classroom.

Also, there's a shared Google Drive folder of ideas for you at tinyurl.com/ISeeMath. Feel free to download any of them and add your own to the folder. Alice Keeler and the late Diana Herrington, authors of *Teaching Math With Google Apps: 50 G Suite Activities* sparked this idea, and Alice continues to regularly contribute to it.

At a recent conference of teachers in Texas, one responded to the I See Math idea with, "I teach math and science. Do you think I See Science would work too?" Great idea! For those of you teaching multiple subjects, you can make your I See _____ an active part of your classroom in all subjects.

Think before you act. My mom often said that to me as I was about to do something questionable, like jump off the high wall of my front porch. If I'd taken the Do Now route instead of the Think Now route at that moment, the outcome may have been entirely different, and likely painful. If you have been using Do Now questions in your classroom, I hope for an entirely different outcome in the future for you and your students. I hope for energy, interest, curiosity, and engagement to set the tone for learning. Students gladly "do now" what they find interesting right now, and the I See Math hack will hook them into the lesson and warm up their minds for mathematical engagement.

PULL A DOUBLE SWITCH AND ADD PRACTICE TIME

Applying best practices for practicing best

I like a teacher who gives you something to take home to think about besides homework.
— LILY TOMLIN, ACTRESS

THE PROBLEM: HOMEWORK IS NOT HELPING STUDENTS LEARN

YOU'VE PROBABLY HEARD of the song by The Notorious B.I.G., "Mo Problems, Mo Money." It's an a cappella choral piece that poetically shares the scientific evidence which backs the claim that the amount of math homework students do per day has a direct impact on the students' salaries over their lifetimes. If you haven't heard the song, that's because it doesn't exist, and neither does the research. What does exist is research that shows traditional math homework (a certain number of problems assigned nightly, after a lesson and about that lesson, which is checked the next day for credit and may be reviewed at the start of class) has little to no significant impact on student achievement. Math homework does, however, correlate strongly to student and family stress, math anxiety, higher incidents of cheating (copying for completion), and long-term dislike of mathematics as a subject.

"But if they're not doing homework, when will our students practice math skills? Aren't they supposed to master certain concepts and skills? I just don't have time in class to teach AND let them do practice problems." You may have heard these statements, and maybe you've even said them yourself. It is time for math teachers to rethink the traditional approach to homework.

Class time is often wasted by ineffective homework-review time. Tell me if this sounds familiar: "OK kids, take out your homework. I'll come around and check it while you do the Do Now problem. Let me know if you have any questions when I come around." You begin walking around the room. [Insert name of boy who never does his homework] looks up at you and says, "Sorry Mr. [insert your name], I didn't do it." You respond, "OK, well if you show it to me tomorrow I'll give you half credit."

You keep walking around the room checking homework for completion when you see [insert name of girl who doesn't want to let you down] copying things down on her paper then handing a worksheet back to her friend, [insert name of girl who's reluctant to share but does anyway]. On your way to deal with the two of them, [insert name of boy who's genuinely interested in learning the math but struggles mightily since he waived up into this higher-level class against his previous teacher's recommendation] catches your attention and points out the seven homework problems he'd like you to go over on the board.

Fifteen to twenty minutes later, you've answered all the questions he had while the other students who didn't need that review sat by and waited. As you begin your lesson, the Do Now is a distant memory, and the homework has taken over the lesson. There's got to be a better way.

THE HACK: PULL A DOUBLE SWITCH AND ADD PRACTICE TIME

The situation I described above is all too familiar to many of us. In fact, it's a part of class that often deteriorates our own motivation for teaching. And while much of the research shows that traditional math homework has little to no effect on achievement in younger grades, the same studies show that as students age, engaging in classwork outside of school can be beneficial to achievement on school-level and state tests. So we need to find the balance.

When I was in fourth grade, I decided to play the alto saxophone. My teacher, Ms. Smith, followed an interesting process when she taught me a new skill like a scale or technique. She would watch intensely, noting and correcting mistakes I was making with my fingerings, my posture, and my tendency to rush when I played. This was active, actionable feedback. She did not, however, assign me that scale for homework. She would say, "We'll look at that scale again next week. Until then, practice the scales we've already tested on to make sure they're still fresh and ready to include in a piece of music. Remember, practice doesn't make perfect. Practice makes permanent." Ms. Smith knew that if I went home and practiced the new scale, I would be practicing incorrect techniques, permanently embedding them in my mental and physical memory, making it difficult to correct them in the future. She made sure that didn't happen.

You can make sure the same thing doesn't happen with your math students with a Double Switch. In baseball, a Double Switch is when the starting pitcher is taken out of the game and the relief pitcher comes in, but instead of being placed in the batting order where the previous pitcher was, the manager moves a current outfielder into the open place in the lineup so that he can bat sooner, and the new pitcher won't have to hit for a while. It's a substitution strategy that gets the most potential result from the switch. That is exactly the purpose of the Double Switch for homework. There are two moves to make: 1. Take the starting pitcher (homework on today's lesson) out of the lineup and move the relief pitcher in (Lagging Homework), but wait to use him for a bit, and 2. In the meantime, bring in someone more valuable (In-Class Practice) to get the best result.

Communicating the message behind the idea will increase buy-in from your students.

In short, make In-Class Practice a major part of your class time. This isn't as much a Hack as it is a procedure and classroom culture shift. When students practice a sport, the coach is there to give feedback. When they practice math, be there to give feedback. Take back the homework review time from the start of class and move it to after a lesson. Like my saxophone teacher, intensely watch your students practice. Listen closely for mistakes. Remind them of what they already know and how they can use it. Then, don't assign more of the same practice for homework, because it may reinforce incorrect work. This shift will change the culture in your classroom from one where students resent practice work to one where students respect its value.

So where does Lagging Homework fit into the Double Switch? The concept, introduced to me by longtime math educator and author Henri Picciotto, completely separates tonight's homework from today's lesson. Instead, give reduced homework based on ideas and topics that were introduced about a week earlier. With Lagging Homework, students don't see the assignment as a task to simply finish on time, and teachers don't rush components of their lessons just to equip their students with the tools to do the homework. We've all done that, but really, when was the last time you wrote that the objective of a lesson was to make sure your students can complete the homework? Never, so why should we make it the hidden objective? Another benefit of Lagging Homework is that students can invest in the learning process without the pressure of the assignment. If a lesson goes over a couple days, that's fine—they're still learning. This gives your lessons time to sink in, develop, and come to fruition—while giving your students time to learn at their own speed, ask questions, and invest in the topic. Give it a shot.

When you combine In-Class Practice with Lagging Homework to create the Double Switch, you've completely viewed mathematics learning from a new perspective. Instead of lecture, self-practice, review, reteach, assess, you've now created an environment where lecture/discovery, collaborative practice and feedback, mastery checks, and alternative assessment can take over and inspire true learning and a more positive perception of math for life.

WHAT YOU CAN DO TOMORROW

Hack 2 is practical and immediately implementable in your classroom the same way the Double Switch happens instantaneously in baseball. It just takes an open mind and an explanation of the process to your students.

- **Take time in class to do today's practice.**
  Start by not assigning homework tonight on

today's lesson, and instead give time for students to practice the work you would have assigned—while they're still in class. Allow students the chance to work together on practice, discuss it, and get coaching and feedback from you before they leave your classroom.

- **During practice, be the coach.** Like great athletic coaches or music teachers, pay attention to your students AS they practice. Listen to their explanations and misconceptions and provide feedback in the form of guiding questions and conceptual directions that help them continue learning, not just find the next step.

- **Tell your students about Lagging Homework.** Communicating the message behind the idea will increase buy-in from your students. They'll be significantly more willing to do the smaller, lagged homework sets if they know their purpose and your intent.

- **Assign practice from last week's learning.** If you're reading this anytime during a school year, start right now by halting assignments based on the daily lesson and assigning Lagging Homework. If you're reading this before the start of the school year, begin right away with the idea.

A BLUEPRINT FOR FULL IMPLEMENTATION

Step 1: Find a clean break to shift homework review time in your class to active practice time.

You've got to create a shifted window for Lagging Homework to take effect. If you're just starting a school year, it's a bit easier since you can create this culture from the get-go. If not, you may have a unit coming to an end that can become a break point to introduce the new structure to your students. Or go ahead and start immediately if you're ready to roll with it right away.

Step 2: Communicate the In-Class Practice and Lagging Homework idea to your students, their parents, and your administration.

At first, some students and others will be confused by the idea of Lagging Homework. Clearly communicate the value of the process. Outline for them that giving students more time to understand a concept increases their ability to successfully complete the homework and that, since more time will be given to the learning process, fewer homework problems will be required for mastery completion. Explain how Lagging Homework gives you the freedom to extend lessons over multiple class periods when necessary, and extends the exposure to a topic over multiple weeks, thereby increasing student time with the concept even further.

Step 3: Keep homework short and accessible.

You'll be off to a great start if the first assignments you give truly model that you are not punishing slower learners with a lot of homework. Look back about a week and see what you taught. Choose a few problems that represent that topic well and assign them as homework this week. It doesn't even matter if the topic is directly related to this week's learning. In fact, it may be better if it isn't; then the assignment will serve the purpose of keeping a recent, but somewhat forgotten, concept fresh in your students' memories. It's the In-Class Practice component that you're using to develop the new skill, not the homework.

Step 4: Create a schedule map to follow for focus.

Implementing these changes doesn't need to create confusion for you or your students, so create a plan for homework that you and your students can understand and predict. After one week of teaching, begin assigning homework on that material at the start of the second week. Put a three- or four-week chart up on the board that labels the progression, clarifying which week you're teaching now, and which week or topic the homework is on. You may also want to include assessments and reassessments in the table so that students know the full scope of your instructional cycle.

Step 5: Change your assessment schedule to include Lagging Homework and revisions.

Your assessment schedule is bound to change if you implement Lagging Homework. You can no longer give students a summative assessment on a math topic right at the end of the topic if they're just beginning their homework on that topic. The week of Lagging Homework will help you identify your students' remaining weaknesses and misconceptions, which you can then address through instruction or supplementary materials. Assessment must now follow that period of time.

I mentioned earlier that I was introduced to the idea of Lagging Homework by Henri Picciotto, who successfully implemented it in his own classroom, and now presents on the topic as well. One of the biggest changes Henri brought along with the In-Class Practice and Lagging Homework model was that his assessment schedule also shifted. He decided not to quiz or test on a topic until several days had been spent on it in homework, and to require quiz corrections, done as homework and counted for points, from every student. This extended the topic over a longer period of time, and emphasized student learning and mastery, not just completion within a set period of time. Here's a version of Henri's schedule, including assessments:

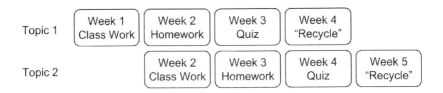

OVERCOMING PUSHBACK

Homework is a sensitive subject for a lot of teachers, administrators, students, and parents. Some love it; some hate it. We're in a time when we are constantly searching for an effective way to engage students in practicing newly acquired skills without anxiety, fear, or stress. But, we're in luck, as the pushback for this hack is mostly about procedure and policy, not concept.

How will I know if my students understood my lesson? That's the purpose of formative assessment. Before making this shift, homework becomes an assessment of the day's lesson, but instead you want homework to do what it was intended to do: Identify what students don't know. If you allow lessons to flow naturally for a few days, your students will have fewer components of the lesson that they don't know, and you'll have fewer parts of the topic to reteach.

We have a grading policy and homework is 10 percent. Won't this inflate their grades if I only assign what they already know? If the purpose of homework in your district is to hold grades down, then yes, this will likely inflate grades. If you're currently grading homework on completion and effort, then no, this will not inflate grades as you're already inflating them with compliance points. The second, and more important response to this concern, is that if an In-Class Practice and Lagging Homework combination is effective in increasing student understanding and achievement in mathematics classrooms, then you now have evidence for a change to the homework policy. Remember, those policies should be determined based on what is best for student learning. Student learning should not be confined by the policies.

I don't have time in class to teach AND let them do practice problems. Here's the beauty of this process: The time you previously spent on homework review is replaced by In-Class Practice of today's problems while you watch, listen, coach, and provide feedback to help them truly master the new concepts.

THE HACK IN ACTION

Henri first wrote about the idea of Lagging Homework on his blog, Math Education Page (mathedpage.org), in 2013. He has been successfully implementing this process in his classroom, giving his students more time to understand a concept, increasing their readiness to do the homework on that topic, and reducing the amount of time "going over the homework" in class.

Since this process also reduces the amount of homework, he can more adequately assess student comprehension of the questions. Also, if he decides to dedicate time to review the homework, students can check with each other much more effectively if there are only a few questions to discuss. (You know how homework checks can revert back to a flurry of writing down correct answers.) If, after students check with each other, a misconception still remains, he creates a new question similar to the problematic one, and engages all students.

Kent Haines, a math teacher in Birmingham, Alabama implemented Lagging Homework for the 2017-2018 school year after looking for a better way to approach homework in his Pre-Algebra and Algebra 1 classes. Now he hands out a practice packet on Monday which covers the material from the week before. Students can schedule when and how they complete the work, as long as they complete it by Friday. Kent shared on Twitter that starting this process was a lot of work up front, but was well worth it since homework was off his plate all week and he was now free to teach at the pace his students needed. From the onset of this process he noticed bigger gains in fluency and comprehension in his students, alongside reduced anxiety.

This model can also be inserted into an existing curriculum. A middle school in my previous district, where I was the Mathematics Supervisor, provides an example of this. The district used the Connected Math series, CMP3, which is an inquiry-based model providing investigations on topics. The investigations are intended to spread over multiple days to allow students time to develop an understanding of the concepts. Unfortunately, these investigations also had homework and practice problems embedded along the way. Fortunately, we decided, as a group, that homework problems would no longer be assigned from current investigations, but only from past, completed investigations. This matched the concept of the inquiry-based program incredibly well. It was much easier to tell students and parents that we wanted them to work through a new concept together, learning and revising their understanding along the way, when we were assigning homework on material that they had the opportunity to fully learn.

What can the Double Switch bring to your classroom and to your students? More time, increased content exposure, reduced stress, greater communication, and appreciation for the work being done, alongside feedback, coaching, and support. If homework is a regular struggle in your classroom because students either have difficulty finding the motivation to do it, or because you're spending too much time going over it in class each day, then both of these issues can be alleviated by adding practice time in class, lagging your homework, and truly focusing on your students' learning and mastery of math.

JOIN THE MDBOS

Bringing the global math teaching community into your classroom

Call it a clan, call it a network, call it a tribe, call it a family. Whatever you call it, whoever you are, you need one.
– JANE HOWARD, AMERICAN JOURNALIST AND AUTHOR

THE PROBLEM: THERE'S NO ONE AT MY SCHOOL INTERESTED IN CHANGE LIKE THIS

IF YOU'RE READING a book called *Hacking Mathematics* and you're a math teacher, then there's little doubt that you're interested in changing the status quo in your classroom and if possible, in your school. Often, teachers feel like they're alone in their quest for better. It may even be true that in your school, small or large, you feel isolated or unsure of where next to take your passion for excellent mathematics education.

For many teachers, this educational unrest usually leads them to the internet to look for creative, new ideas. In an unfortunate number of cases, though, teachers end up on Teachers Pay Teachers (TPT) or Pinterest, digging through sellable and decorative lessons. You may filter through them and find the occasional gem, like Cathy Yenca and her MathyCathy page on TPT. She has excellent resources that thousands of math teachers have adopted, but still, even at their most valuable, the resources are PDFs and basic instructions. If you want real learning, real personal experience, then don't look for the resources. Look for the actual source: math teacher blogs.

THE HACK: JOIN THE MTBOS

The what? The MTBoS. It's an acronym for the Math Twitter Blog-o-Sphere, a community of math teachers who blog about their teaching and who also have Twitter accounts where they regularly share their blog posts and ideas. Search Twitter for #MTBoS and you'll find an instant community of passionate teachers who can help you with everything from how to use a digital tool in your classroom to how to find a better way to promote intrinsic motivation in your students regarding Riemann sums.

Many of the teachers in the #MTBoS get together at the summer conference I mentioned earlier called Twitter Math Camp. With no corporate sponsorship or vendor areas for free pens and stress balls, approximately two hundred math teachers gather and answer the question, "How can we all help each other be better, more effective math teachers?" We've shared ideas, created activities, curated resources, and most of all, we've become a family. You're not alone, and now you know where to find your clan.

WHAT YOU CAN DO TOMORROW

This one doesn't take a lot of convincing or outside-of-the-box thinking. Follow these simple steps and you'll be ready to go.

- **Sign up for Twitter.** If you don't already have a Twitter account, stop reading (not now; at the end of this bullet point), open your phone or computer, and start an account as your teacher self (keep that in mind when choosing your Twitter handle). If you already have a professional Twitter account, GREAT. If you only have a personal one, change it to a professional account or create a new one if you want to keep both.
- **Type #MTBoS in the search bar.** You'll see tweets using the hashtag, and you'll see teachers who are tweeting. You can click

on the "people" tab as well, and see more teachers currently using the hashtag. Follow all of them and follow who they follow.

- **Visit the MTBoS website, mtbos.org**. Here you'll find a directory of members, links to their blogs to start your reading, the top resources, and the best ways to connect. Remember, all of this was done voluntarily by teachers who care deeply about students learning math and who want the best for their students. You know, teachers like you.

- **Start a blog.** This is the big step. Having a blog is not a prerequisite for being a part of the MTBoS, but you'll find that sharing is most definitely caring, and that many can benefit from your thoughts, as much as you can from theirs. You'll find that your blog becomes an outlet for your creativity and your frustration, and a place to share what you're trying, or thinking about trying. The #MTBoS is there with you and will read, encourage, support, and simply help you grow. You can do the same.

A BLUEPRINT FOR FULL IMPLEMENTATION

Step 1: Engage strongly with the #MTBoS Twitter community.

Signing up for Twitter is one thing. Coming up with a catchy handle that hasn't already been taken (like @MathDenisNJ), updating your profile picture and banner, and sending that first tweet are all very exciting and sometimes nerve-wracking aspects of the task. But that can only take you so far. The Math Twitter Blog-o-Sphere is eager to meet new members, so reach out and say hello. Then, ask questions and include the hashtag. Answer questions you see others asking. If you're going to a conference, tweet about it and see who's there. Meet up if you can and put real faces with names.

> **Harness the amazing connections you now have at your fingertips by becoming part of an exciting and caring group of educators. You can learn from others, and others can learn from you, and students will reap the benefits.**

If you're ready to up your Twitter game, go to tweet-deck.com and log in with your Twitter account. Type the #MTBoS hashtag into the search and add a column to add it to your new favorite Twitter tool. On TweetDeck, you can see everyone's tweets and comments without having to search every time. It's the perfect way to become a part of the day-to-day lives of the community. I did this three years ago and it changed my math teaching forever, and reinvigorated my passion for math education in ways I never could have imagined.

Step 2: Read all the blogs.

Maybe not all of them, but get started reading. You bought this book, so clearly you're on board with reading. You can start reading from the blog directory, or, if you'd like a more targeted approach, just ask your Twitter community which blog to read for your content area. I'll even give you your first tweet. "Hi #MTBoS. I'm new and excited to learn from everyone. Which blogs do you recommend for a (insert content area here) teacher?" That's it. Feel free to tweet that one; it's not copyrighted.

Step 3: Start your blog and get writing.

There's no MToS. Just an MTBoS, with blogs included. Are you wondering what you should blog about? We've all had that same thought. Often, we put off blogging because the idea we have isn't perfect, or isn't fully worked out, or the lesson isn't finished, or our post is just not as well-written as we'd hoped. Those are the exact reasons TO blog. You need to put out imperfect ideas, because we're all imperfect and learning together. You need to blog about lessons as they happen, unfinished and in progress. Those reflections and perspectives matter. And seriously, write whether it's well-written or not. I've yet to meet a math teacher who judges the literary value of another's blog post. We want to learn from you, and we can't if you don't share your moments with us.

OVERCOMING PUSHBACK

There are three types of pushback that come from joining the #MTBoS: the internal, the external, and the familial. Here's how to manage all three.

Internal: I'm not sure I have any reason to do this. Ah, the internal struggle of self-worth in the math teaching community. Unless you spend your Twitter and blog time focusing on tearing down others for their ideas and comments, then you do have a reason to do this. Your questions raise questions for others and validate the questions we might have at the same time. If your input affects one other teacher positively, then you have a reason to do this. If you gain one good idea or positive affirmation from another teacher, then you have a reason to do this.

External: My school administration and colleagues don't think I should be writing about my students. Your school administration and colleagues are wrong, or simply don't understand the intent. However, in the interest of student safety in our digital world, make sure to follow all school district protocol and policies. If students have signed a waiver that their images or works can be included in school publications, then social media posts are usually included in that. You can also approach your posts with anonymity by removing identifying characteristics of your school, not using student names or full names, not showing student faces, or by putting emojis over student faces. If you're writing about your lessons, you should be fine. That's general and can only enhance your teaching. If you've got a very sensitive administration and community, then bring the idea of a blog and Twitter to your principal and have an open discussion. Good leaders will encourage teachers who want good things for their students.

Familial: My wife/husband/significant other doesn't get it. I'm married and have four kids. Those five other people do not afford me much free time in my home to get together online with my #MTBoS clan. When I first began, I told my wife what I was going to do and had her read a lot of my blog posts because I love her and value her input. She still reads my posts, but not before I post them. There were plenty of times when she'd ask why I was on my phone so much, but that subsided when she saw my excitement grow for teaching math. Be open about your need for this community and what it brings to your career and happiness, and make time when you can. Know when the regular math Twitter chats are held, check TweetDeck frequently in small bursts so you don't have to spend a big chunk of time on it, and unplug for your family. The MTBoS understands.

THE HACK IN ACTION

I started blogging in late 2014. I joined Twitter at the same time, and came across the MTBoS in the spring of 2015. At that time, I also heard about Twitter Math Camp, which was to be held in California. I proposed a session and was accepted to speak at TMC15, which was an incredibly exciting moment for me. First, I hadn't been to California in fifteen years, and also, I would get to learn in person from the excellent educators I'd been learning from on Twitter for the past months.

I signed up to be part of a Project Based Learning morning session that would be held over all three days of the conference. The session was run by Mary Bourassa and Alex Overwijk. Day three of the session was supposed to be a time for all of us to plan activities further, but as we'd been talking over the previous two days, it became apparent that we all had regular activities and that the time could be better spent collectively sharing them. Mary and Alex took the cue and ran with it, redirecting their session to a curation workshop instead. We collaborated on creating a spreadsheet of activities and shared it with the Twitter Math Camp participants and the #MTBoS. (You can find that spreadsheet at tinyurl. com/mtbosPBL)

This type of situation is the heart of the Math Twitter Blog-o-Sphere. If an idea is good for teaching and learning math, even if it's unplanned, then we're willing to follow it down that road and get the most from it.

It's not unusual to feel alone in schools today. Email and internet technology have made it possible to be confined to your classroom without meeting other teachers much at all. There are teachers who are satisfied to keep following the lesson plans they've used for the past ten years to teach students for the next ten, but I have a feeling that you're not satisfied with that. Harness the amazing connections you now have at your fingertips by becoming part of an exciting and caring group of educators. You can learn from others, and others can learn from you, and students will reap the benefits. Your enthusiasm for participating in the global math community may just be the thing that sparks a new interest throughout your own school, too.

ENCOURAGE A DIGITAL SHOW AND TELL

Using a 1:1 environment to demonstrate understanding

You're thinking about something, my dear,
and that makes you forget to talk.
— LEWIS CARROLL, WRITER, MATHEMATICIAN, AND AUTHOR
OF *ALICE'S ADVENTURES IN WONDERLAND*

THE PROBLEM: KIDS DON'T KNOW HOW TO SHOW MATH WORK DIGITALLY

WHEN YOU'VE WRITTEN instructions for students, there's a chance you've included the phrase "show your work" at the end. Up until the advent of the 1:1 classroom—where each student has access to his or her own digital technology device such as a laptop or tablet—that instruction was easy for students to follow. They just needed to show all their steps so we could grade them according to our particular point-based rubric, and so we could circle mistakes for them to review later.

Now many of our classrooms have Chromebooks, laptops, or iPads in order to keep up with 21st century learning standards and prepare our students for a world that will always include technology. Herein lies the conflict. Showing work used to be simple, but if we want the same type of result from that instruction now, our students need to become experts at writing mathematics with equation editors, such as LaTeX, and that means not coming up with a better way themselves. Many students prefer finding their own ways to solve problems, and one student said something to me that changed "show your work" for the better.

THE HACK: ENCOURAGE A DIGITAL SHOW AND TELL

My son, Danny, is in first grade, and it was his turn to bring in an item for show and tell one week. I asked him what he wanted to bring in, and he chose a small bag of "gems" that I'd brought home for him from a recent trip to South Dakota. The gems were just polished rocks with which, for the low, low price of $5.99, I could fill a small velvety bag to the top. Danny likes rocks, so that was the perfect souvenir (French for "remember to throw this out later") for him from my trip. As he held the little bag of gems, I asked him what he would say about it in class the next day.

Seventeen minutes later, my fatherly ears now filled with

geological adjectives, Danny finished answering that question. He took out each rock, showed it to me, described what he liked about it, branched off to talk about how similar a particular rock was to an object in a video game he played or a book he'd read, and made sure I was listening by checking in regularly with, "Do you like this too, Dad?"

If I'd asked him to write down what he wanted to say to his class, it would have ended after one sentence of what likely would have been average grammar and subpar penmanship. That's because writing what he's thinking isn't natural to Danny yet. He's not able to create the letters, words, and sentences efficiently and proficiently enough to make writing explanations a viable tool for him. So instead, Danny talks.

> ## When you change the instruction from "show your work" to "explain your thinking," you offer students the opportunity to do this by whatever means they are most comfortable.

And that day in class, what my student said to me was, "Instead of typing math, can I just tell you what I did?" This is where the 1:1 digital environment thrives. Chromebooks, laptops, and iPads all have one thing in common: They can record voices at the click of a button. There are numerous apps and websites that make this possibility seamless, safe, and effective. You just have to know where to find them.

WHAT YOU CAN DO TOMORROW

Teachers have been creating and sharing videos for a long time. We've been flipping our classes, using Khan Academy, and finding instructional videos on YouTube and Vimeo as they become increasingly available and instructionally valuable in our classrooms. How can you leverage these as tools for your students to explain their work and show you their thinking?

- **Let your students talk in class.** They may not be used to this, but it's what they want to do. I've seen a classroom poster that says, "You have two ears and one mouth so you can listen twice as much as you speak." What teachers need to realize is that the message is meant for them, not for students. The more comfortable students become talking to each other about their solutions, questions, and ideas, the easier it will be for them to express themselves to you.

- **Try Flipgrid.** Go to flipgrid.com and sign up for a free trial. It's an easy video interface for your students that doesn't require any logins for kids and can range from totally private to fully open, depending on how you set it up. It's available as a web-based tool for laptops and

Chromebooks or as a smartphone app. This one's a game changer.

- **Enable screen recording on devices.** iPhones and iPads have the capability to record their screens while simultaneously recording a person narrating. When you make this feature available on classroom iPads or personal devices, students can begin using them to "show and tell" their mathematical explanations.

- **Remove the "show your work" instruction.** Swap this out for "explain your thinking" as often as possible. Students can do that without knowing how to create mathematical equations in Word or a Google Doc.

A BLUEPRINT FOR FULL IMPLEMENTATION

Step 1: Read about promoting mathematical discourse.

It would be presumptuous to assume that just because we want our students to discuss mathematics in our classrooms, they're going to be instantly able to do it productively with comfort and ease. You will want to familiarize yourself with the types of feedback, questions, and comments you can provide that will promote discourse among your students. This will teach them how to interact in their mathematical discussions, how to build on and refute each other's mathematical claims, and how to communicate their ideas and solutions with clarity. An excellent place to start is a white paper from the Math Forum which can be found at tinyurl.com/MFdiscourse. You can also find 100 Questions That Promote Mathematical Discourse at tinyurl.com/100discourse.

Step 2: Encourage students to create brief video explanations with Flipgrid.

Flipgrid is a web-based or app-based format for short videos. In fact, participants are limited to thirty-, sixty-, or ninety-second clips. The teacher can ask a question through video or writing, and students are given a code to enter the grid topic and create their own short video responses. Student logins are not necessary. I've seen many teachers using Flipgrid for exit tickets, short performances, and project pitches. You can hack this for your math class by asking students to complete problems or tasks on paper, then have them explain their solutions while literally "showing their work" to the camera. If students don't like their videos, it's one click and they can redo it. This allows them to listen to their own responses, decide whether or not they were clear, and revise their explanations if necessary.

Step 3: Highlight creative student-based methods.

When you change the instruction from "show your work" to "explain your thinking," you offer students the opportunity to do this by whatever means they are most comfortable. It may be via Flipgrid or another screencasting tool. They may record their voices into a recorder app and create an explanation that they can then share with you. In most cases, students have varying comfort levels with different types of technology and will naturally gravitate toward those that are most comfortable for them. When students share new ways of explaining their thinking, it's time for you to share those creative methods with all students, other teachers, and even the online community via Twitter.

OVERCOMING PUSHBACK

Every change to an established system will have its fair share of naysayers. Here are a few ways to address their concerns.

If students only verbalize their thinking, they won't be able to show their work on the SATs or state assessments. The common misconception here is that students will ONLY speak their explanations, and thereby lose their abilities to write solutions well. However, students are using the verbalization process to create initial explanations, then work on revisions, then finalize explanations that are concise and correct. Once students reach this point, they are encouraged to write their conclusions and, once again, show their work. The difference this time is that their work is clear and free from unnecessary developmental thoughts. Once their thoughts and solutions reach this point, teaching them how to use standardized test assessment writing programs is easy. When they don't understand the math, the software gets in the way.

I know students who just won't do this. Are they the same students who don't want to do their homework, anyway? It may be surprising to hear that students who are usually reluctant to engage in classroom conversation are much more likely to share their own thoughts and explanations if they're able to do it privately or individually. After trying this in your classroom, you'll have examples to share with this type of naysayer, possibly even from individual students who were once in the naysayer's class, and this can serve as the best proof that this process works.

I'm not sure how to grade this kind of work. There are a few approaches to this. One is simple: Don't grade it until it's final. Don't give partial credit for explanations that need revisions—just ask for revisions. Don't give partial credit for seventy-second videos when you wanted ninety seconds. It just wouldn't make sense. But when you ask students for an assessment of their learning and expect their best, most refined, most exact explanation, that's when you may decide to grade it. The other approach is to have students self-evaluate what they've shared. Grade their effort in self-evaluation, not on the math. This will value the time they put into their learning as much as the content that they're learning over time.

THE HACK IN ACTION

Having students explain their thinking to you verbally, rather than writing it, can be a challenge. Robert McFail, fourth-grade math and science teacher from McKinney Independent School District in Texas, has incorporated Flipgrid in various ways with his students. He posts a "must do" question to be completed by the end of the week, and students post their solutions and explanations. He also asks students to use Flipgrid to teach him how to solve a problem or to analyze his solution and look for mistakes. Rob will even ask them to tell him, through the video platform, "things that make sense, and things that you're still struggling with." Based on the responses to his grids, Rob's students are excited to share their ideas, comment on each other's work, and teach as often as they learn.

Other ways to take advantage of Flipgrid and screen recording apps include having students create help videos for each other. When students want to know more about the app itself or about another non-instructional aspect of the course, they can post questions and receive responses from other students in the classroom. You don't always have to answer all the questions just because you're the teacher. You can also ask your students to create assessment questions for their classmates to answer. With Flipgrid's response feature, you can view responses before posting them, so you don't have to worry about other students copying a response. You can also address any issues through direct comments to students.

While making the shift to creating and viewing videos can take time, many teachers I've talked to share the point that student eagerness overcomes teacher workload. Sooner, rather than later, students are taking the reins and looking for opportunities to express their mathematical thinking. This leads to more time in class to discuss what students need, and less time marking papers just to show what they did.

I dare you to tell me this hasn't been a conversation in your classroom:

You: Show me what you did for Problem 5.

Student: I got 2x + 3.

You: That's not totally correct, but you didn't show your work, so I don't know what you were thinking when you solved it. Tell me how you did it.

This Hack knocks out the middleman and the wasted time. Go straight to hearing how your students did their work and what they were thinking when they were doing it. Make show and tell part of your math classroom every day.

BE LESS HELPFUL AND ASK MORE QUESTIONS

Turning mathematical struggles into deep learning

I'm sorry, but your answer must be in the form of a question.
— ALEX TREBEK, JEOPARDY! GAME SHOW HOST

THE PROBLEM: MATH TEACHERS ARE TOO HELPFUL

IT'S TRUE. MATH teachers want nothing more than for their students to have an enjoyable experience learning math so that they don't become the future "I hate math" people like the ones permeating the public sphere today. To stave off the hatred and bad feelings toward mathematics, we help. We help students when they ask questions. We help students before they ask questions, thinking they'll have the same questions as the previous students. We help students with their homework and practice. We are notorious for providing "extra help" before school, during lunch, after school, and during planning periods despite, or sometimes negotiated into, our contracts. But in all of this time, are we actually helping kids learn math, or are we just helping them complete mathematical procedures, memorize mathematical information, and demonstrate mathematical retention?

Why is this a problem? Aren't students entitled to help when they need it? Don't we want to create frustration-free, positive environments in our classrooms? The answer to both of these questions is yes ... and no. Students are entitled to help when they need it, but do you know when they need it or are you just helping when they say they need it? Are frustration-free classrooms and positive learning environments good? Of course they are, but can you tell the difference between frustration and productive struggle, or the difference between positive learning experiences and positive feelings? There is a solution to this problem: Question everything.

THE HACK: BE LESS HELPFUL AND ASK MORE QUESTIONS

When you have the opportunity to visit math classrooms in different schools as often as I do, you see a lot of situations that look like TV shows you've watched. Some look like ER, where triage is key, and teachers are in an all-out frenzy to help everyone as quickly as possible, sometimes even with a team of teachers on the job. Other classrooms look like game shows, only the host is the one answering questions with short, factual answers before moving on to the next question. I'm sure you have more television-related analogies of your own to add here.

But none of our students are mathematically bleeding out. None need mathematical hospitalization or algebraic surgery. And none of us has more mathematical facts to spew than does the internet. This is why we need to stop being math doctors and fact machines. Instead, we need to question everything.

> **Our students are learning math along a conceptual pathway that needs time to develop. That development needs your questions, not your answers.**

When a student raises his hand and says, "I don't know what to do in this problem," don't tell him what to do, question him. "What have you tried so far?"

When a student raises her hand and says, "Did I get this one right?" don't check it, question her. "How can you tell if your answer is correct?"

When a student looks confused but hasn't asked a question, don't analyze his work and point to the next step, question him. "What do you notice about this question? What do you think is the question that you need to answer?"

Every time you're ready to give a mathematical answer, or point to a mathematical procedure, or remind of a previous example, or begin reteaching a mathematical concept, stop. Ask a question instead, then give your students time to think about and answer it. Make your classroom more like the concept behind the game show Jeopardy! Give all your answers in the form of a question.

WHAT YOU CAN DO TOMORROW

Retraining yourself to ask questions instead of giving answers may take time, but you can begin integrating this Hack instantly, with a little awareness and a few prompts for yourself. Your students might need a little training, too.

- **Plan tomorrow's questions.** You're teaching something tomorrow, or reviewing something, or testing on something. Look at your plan, your review, or your assessment and think about the questions your students are most likely to ask. Now, plan a response that is another question that can redirect them toward a better understanding of their current strategy. Get them to think.

- **Ask questions that don't have answers.** In Hack 1, I mentioned using I See Math as a way to warm up for class. The great thing about I See Math questions is that they don't have one final answer. As often as possible, add questions like these to engage thinking and to develop follow-up questions.

- **Rebrand your extra help sessions.** Tell students that extra help time is not going to be quick answers to easy questions. Students should come to you with a need and be prepared to get questions to answer, not answers to their questions.

A BLUEPRINT FOR FULL IMPLEMENTATION

Step 1: Enlist your colleagues.

This is not a Hack that needs a team of teachers to implement it in order to be successful, but it is one that will benefit from collective feedback. When you and other teachers implement this Hack in your classes, and then take time to discuss the results and the types and effectiveness of questions you're asking on a daily basis, you grow as a team and you help your students.

Step 2: Teach your students to ask themselves questions.

As you ask questions to your students, they may or may not notice that you're trying a new strategy as you approach their learning. If they don't notice, and I guess even if they do, it's a good practice to tell them what you've done after you've done it. Say, "When you don't know how to begin a problem, ask yourself 'What do I notice about the question?'" This can build capacity in your students and remove the dependency on you to ask those probing questions. Encourage them to ask each other similar questions when working in small groups.

Step 3: Commit to questioning everything.

Our students are learning math along a conceptual pathway that needs time to develop. That development needs your questions, not your answers. For a time, not answering student questions may feel wrong, or even like you're not helping them learn enough. That's just not true. Your questions are helping them continue along the conceptual pathway and internalize it for the future. Your answers were just street signs and traffic lights along the way. They came and went without a lasting impression.

Step 4: Reflect on your questioning.

Did you ask a question that confused a student? Was that because of the way you asked the question, the nature of the question itself, or something else? Can you be more prepared to ask leading, learning questions? What were the best questions you asked? How do you know they worked? Notice anything about reflecting? It's all questions.

Step 5: Revisit upcoming lesson and unit plans with questions in mind.

Maybe you're the type of teacher who creates new lesson plans every year. If so, then as you plan, put yourself in the shoes of your students, think the way they think, and come up with a list of questions your plan may ignite in them. Then, create your response questions and be ready to share them. Maybe instead, you're the type who trusts the good old tried-and-true plans you've used in the past. If so, dust them off and look at them with fresh eyes like the teacher who plans newly every year. Or maybe you're the type of teacher who thinks they've got it all together enough to not need plans. If so, it's time to begin planning again, and this time make it about questions that will help you direct the learning, and not about content you need to deliver.

OVERCOMING PUSHBACK

Despite the short- and long-term value of asking questions in a math classroom, there will undoubtedly be pushback from students and parents. Here are the most prevalent objections and how to address them.

Why won't you just tell me what to do? This one will come from a student who is in a hurry, or from a student who's not really interested in learning, but just wants to complete the math work. It may also come from a student who genuinely thinks that they only need one more hint or one more step from you, and that will be what pushes them over the top to be able to finish the problem. For the students in a hurry or who don't really care, we have to tell them that we're not in a hurry, that we do care, and that our questions are aimed at making sure they learn, not just do. If we just wanted to order things around and make them do what we told them to do, we'd program robots, not teach children. To the interested, eager, but misguided student, we need to have a reassuring presence that shows them we're interested in making sure they don't need our help every time. These students are most likely to learn how to ask themselves questions during the learning process.

Why aren't you helping when my child comes in with questions? This one will come from a parent of one of the three types of students mentioned in the previous objection. You can offer the same responses to parents that you gave to their children. It may be necessary to share your strategies with parents, as they tend to ask more questions associated with teaching and grading. Remember, though, that they are not professional educators (a few are, but not many) and that we are not instructing them in how to teach, nor are we instructing them to be our teaching assistants at home, nor are we teaching them the math that we're teaching their children. When we share our methods and strategies, we often have to do it firmly, so be ready to support your work using the answers to the reflection questions above and your planning.

Are your students just teaching themselves now? This may come from students, parents, other teachers, or administrators. This Hack is not a call to shift to a full inquiry-based learning model. This is what you do when your students have questions after instruction and during practice. No, your students won't be teaching themselves, but they will be discovering that they can learn more by themselves than they thought. You're still teaching and assessing according to best practice and school policies, but you've shifted the conversation away from helping students finish math to guiding students while they learn math.

THE HACK IN ACTION

Amanda Napolitano, eighth-grade math teacher in Chatham, New Jersey, models this with her algebra students. Much of the algebra course enters into the abstract, less-concrete view of mathematics. Up to this point, students have been learning mathematical operations, formulas, tools, procedures, and more concrete math skills that can be put into use now, which makes Algebra 1 class an excellent time to question everything. In Amanda's algebra class, when students have a hard time beginning a problem, she asks questions like, "What do you know? What do you need to find out? Have you solved similar problems before?"

When students are stuck while working, she asks, "Can you draw a picture to help you see the problem? Can you describe what you've done up to this point? Can you predict what would happen if you tried ...?"

When students aren't sure if they've finished correctly, Amanda asks, "Have you answered the question? Can you convince me that your answer makes sense?"

Questions like these will guide instruction further along the learning pathway and not cut off the conceptual understanding process. They are also generic enough that they can apply to students at different points in their journeys, and naturally meet them where they are, taking their learning from that point forward.

You may not have thought of yourself as too helpful, or even taken pride in how helpful you were. That's OK. Hopefully what you've gained from this Hack is not that helping your students is a bad thing, but that there is another way to help your students learn that doesn't involve answering all their questions, and instead involves asking them questions. Professor David Cooperrider wrote, "We live in worlds our questions create," and I believe that. Questions lead to investigation and a desire to learn. Answers close the door. Again, I offer you this hacky suggestion: Question everything.

GO PROSPECTING FOR RELEVANT LEARNING

Making mathematics real and increasing student engagement

We have no choice but to make learning more relevant to our students, or they will learn without us.
— Denis Sheeran, Author of *Instant Relevance, Using Today's Experiences to Teach Tomorrow's Lessons*

THE PROBLEM: KIDS DON'T WANT TO LEARN MATH

THAT'S NOT TRUE, you say? Kids really DO want to learn math? Maybe they do, but they don't want to learn the math that many of us are teaching to them. When was the last time you had kids run into your classroom begging for more factoring problems? Have you ever been observed while teaching, and then received an evaluation report that said you need to tone down the student engagement? If our students really, honestly wanted to learn math, then we wouldn't be hunting for real-world math problems and cool activities that connect math with life, or assigning projects we think the kids will like. If math was as intrinsically interesting to most of our students as it is to us, half of Pinterest and two-thirds of Teachers Pay Teachers would not exist.

This makes me think of an interesting math question. If I randomly find an activity online, and the fractions I just mentioned about Pinterest and Teachers Pay Teachers are true, what's the probability that the activity is on Pinterest but NOT on TPT? See? I just did it. I felt the need to make math more interesting by asking a probability question with the context. Our students crave the context. They want to know that the math we're teaching is going to be useful in the real world someday, and that it came from somewhere interesting or necessary or mysterious. We can give them that in a much more powerful way than just doing the application problems at the end of the homework section. We can make it real for our students. (Feel free to join me on Twitter for thirty minutes every Wednesday at 9:30 p.m. EST, as we #MakeItReal.)

THE HACK: GO PROSPECTING FOR RELEVANT LEARNING

Relevant math questions and content exist all around us—you just have to know where to look. And actually, you don't need to know where to look, you just have to start looking somewhere and it won't be long before you see opportunities to extract math questions from everyday moments. I did just that in my example above, and I didn't even have a probability question in mind before I started writing the intro to this chapter. I could have moved on and just kept writing, the same way we often see something interesting but walk right past it. Instead, I pulled a probability question out of it.

A third-grade teacher might have asked which website has the larger fraction of math activities. A fourth-grade teacher may have pretended that the two websites were merging and asked for the fraction of the new website that is filled with math activities. A 1:1 classroom could investigate whether the statement was true and back it up with mathematical evidence. There are a lot of possibilities for questions, and even greater examples are all around us.

I call this Hack Go Prospecting for Relevant Learning because I hope you start to view yourself and your students as on the hunt for valuable math out there. In some cases, you'll be able to find it easily, like panning in a river full of gold nuggets. Other times, you're going to have to dig deeper to see it, but you may find a mine full. There might even be times where you need to blow up the side of a metaphorical mountain to see the math in there, but the mother lode is waiting for you below the rubble. So go prospecting. Look around you; look at your life, hobbies, and interests. Look at the weather and other common experiences you share with your students. Look at TV and music. Look at large-scale events like the Olympics and elections and the Fidget Spinner Craze of 2017.

Become great at listening to your students speak so you know when to prospect the gold mines of their perspectives and interests.

WHAT YOU CAN DO TOMORROW

First, when kids ask you when they're going to use this in real life, you can stop saying things like, "On the test next week" or "If you become an engineer" or "Maybe never, but I'm also teaching you critical thinking skills." None of those satisfy the student who actually is interested in why math is important. Here are ways you can make math more relevant and engaging so that the aforementioned question won't need to be answered because it's not being asked anymore.

- **Shoot first, ask questions later.** By which I mean shoot photos and let them serve as catalysts for questions. Like I mentioned in Hack 1, when you see math, say math. Taking pictures and videos of situations you find mathematically interesting, or even ones that just have a dusting of math, but enough to spark a good discussion, will put you on a fast path to creating more engaging math questions for your students.

- **Share what's current.** As I write this, the U.S. government is debating tax reform, health care, and Russian hacking—but even more important, the NCAA College Football Playoff rankings are being thrown into a tizzy by top teams losing unexpectedly. I can tell you this: Some of your students would do anything to engage in a good political conversation, and others would passionately preach about why their team should be in the playoffs. There's a lot of math in both of those situations. Go digging.

- **Find out what makes your students tick.** Your students will be more interested in math related to your life and experiences than they will be about math from their textbooks, because they have a relationship with you and care about you. They will be even more interested in math related to themselves than in math related to you. Find out about their interests, hobbies, favorite shows, current music, and passions, and exploit them for your mathematical gain.

- **Read *Instant Relevance*.** Sure, this sounds like a shameless plug for my other book, but in it I describe seven ways you can increase relevance in your classroom that can take you beyond the Hack.

- **Investigate the 3-Act Math format.** 3-Act Math tasks range from short questions to full lessons based around real situations that may be relevant to you and your students. More importantly, investigate the structure of the tasks and begin to create your own for a significantly more relevant learning experience. You can find them online at denissheeran. com/3-act-math.

A BLUEPRINT FOR FULL IMPLEMENTATION

Step 1: Sell it to your students.

Any time a new product comes around, its longevity is made or broken by the sales pitch. I saw an ad for a kids' science kit that gets delivered to your house once a month and has what looked like unique and cool experiments for you and your kids to do together. But then it happened. In the ad, one of the parents walked around the corner with the new science box, smiled expectantly, and kneeled as the kids rushed up for a big hug, because, you know, YAY, their new science kit was here ... Sorry, as a father of four, the ad didn't resonate with me because I know that the real scene would either be much more like hyenas tearing up a freshly fallen giraffe, or a wave of teenage indifference. The sales pitch of hugs, smiles, and family chemistry time turned me off as too fake, despite my initial interest in the product.

Develop a sales pitch that will make your students want to buy into the "product" of relevant math. This is usually done by good storytelling. You don't have to be Shakespeare; you've just got to know how to tell a story without making it all mathy right away. If you've got an idea from a photo or video or experience that you want to turn into a great math question, plan the story so that the kids are the ones who get around to asking the question. Bait the hook, don't toss dynamite into the pond. They'll take the bait.

Step 2: Start as small as you need to and gradually increase.

Maybe you're the type of teacher who's married to the pacing guide, till death or a new textbook do you part. You may feel the struggle of wondering where you're supposed to fit these types of questions and activities into your already packed schedule. Take out a useless part; that's where you find the time. Andrew Stadel (@MrStadel) has a great talk on the classroom clock and how we spend too much of our time on things that should take up almost no time at all. Evaluate your classroom clock and see what you can sacrifice to make space for more relevant topics. Then try it.

If you're recently or long-since divorced from your pacing guide, and time isn't a problem, then you may be ready for more right away. Start with stories from your experiences that lead to good math questions. Become great at listening to your students speak so you know when to prospect the gold mines of their perspectives and interests. I firmly believe that you could remake a full math course curriculum with questions you discover day by day.

Step 3: Document what you've done and save the good ones.

If you've found an excellent experience, photo, video, location, or mystery that you realize has led to an excellent math experience in your class, document it and include it in your classes for as long as it is relevant. Earlier I mentioned the Fidget Spinner Craze of 2017. Yeah, that's over now, and you might not want to mention it in your classes. But on the other side, I went to New York City to hear my wife sing, and I saw a twenty-six-foot-tall cube with a cylinder cut out of the center of it. It's the Red Cube sculpture by artist Isamu Noguchi, and it was installed in the 1960s. After taking a picture of it, I showed it to students in elementary, middle, and high school and heard the best questions. Where is it? Why is it there? How big is it? How much red paint is on it? How many little snap cubes would it take to fill it? Can we make one of our own?

By letting students investigate, they estimated, calculated area and volume, and used the Pythagorean theorem and quadratic formula to figure out how to make one. That is a story and a lesson that I can repeat. The cube has been there for fifty years and doesn't look like it's going to disappear with fidget-spinner-like speed, so I documented it and put it in my lesson plans for next year. You don't always have to have a new idea to have a relevant learning opportunity. Save the good ones.

Step 4: Enlist your students.

Let's hope that by now your students are on board. If so, then they're beginning to experience the situational awareness effect. That's when you start to see things you never saw before, just because you've been made aware of them. Like if I told you that my lucky number is twenty-two, which it is, you might start seeing twenty-twos everywhere, like on license plates, street signs, price tags, and UPC symbols. It's a whole new world of twenty-twos ... (I apologize for your upcoming twenty-two experiences). If your students are seeing things your way, they'll have ideas, pictures, videos, and mysteries to add to your library. Let them. If you have twenty or a hundred and twenty students, you now have a small army of mathematical noticers who can make their own learning experiences more relevant and engaging.

OVERCOMING PUSHBACK

Your students will likely embrace relevant learning. If you get any pushback, it will come from other teachers or administrators who may be skeptical about any change involving how time is spent in the classroom. Here's what to say in response.

These lessons don't fit into our curriculum. The curriculum is the lessons and materials you use to teach the content of your course. It is not the lessons and materials you *already have* for teaching the content of your course. In math, substitution is when you take one thing out of an expression or equation and substitute in a different thing of equal value. You've probably taught that concept to your kids. Now model it by taking out a lesson you already have and substituting it with content that's more relevant.

The kids won't buy it. This is potentially true if you start creating problems with what Dan Meyer (@ddmeyer) calls pseudo-context. That's when you take math and slap it on top of real-world situation, like telling your students that a whale tail looks like two congruent triangles, or that if they saw a fire coming out of an eight-story window that they'd instantly know the angle of elevation from their eyes to the window and then, after walking twenty feet closer to the burning building, they'd stop and look up again for some reason and also instantly know the angle of elevation to the window, and after all of that time watching a building burn they'd most likely wonder how tall the building was. You know, pseudo-context. Your kids will buy real relevance if the topic is real to them, like the Bottle Flipping Craze of 2016.

Eight out of every ten teachers I know had banned water bottles from the classroom and made bottle flipping a school-level misdemeanor. The other two recognized that their students wanted to do one thing and one thing only … flip bottles. They turned it into a statistics lesson on measuring the probability of different types of bottles with different water levels to determine which was the optimal combination for landing a water bottle, thereby turning their students into lunchroom heroes. I even brought bottle flipping into calculus, using the simple fact that it was a craze. I had students bring in a water bottle of their choice for us to draw and model as a piecewise function, and then we calculated the volume of the water bottle as a 3-D solid of revolution. The best part was that to see if they were right, they just had to look at the side of the bottle. And in the meantime, we heard thuds next to students' seats. No punishment necessary, just a love for the discipline.

There's no way I can do this every day. That is correct, for now. Some lessons are best introduced with a big, relevant mathematical situation that students can chew on over time as the fuel for learning a topic. Others are best served as dessert after a full meal's worth of instruction. The water bottle flipping question was not planned for the first day after hearing about water bottle flipping. Teachers saw an opportunity for a relevant connection to student interests and found a timely place for it in the near future, knowing that fads and trends die quickly among teens. You don't have to rattle your curriculum cage and teach content randomly because you come across a relevant topic. Instead, find the time to make that lesson most relevant to your students and your course.

THE HACK IN ACTION

I've already provided a few examples of this Hack in action, such as the Pinterest/TPT problem, the Red Cube Question, and the Fidget Spinner and Bottle Flipping Crazes. There are many other stories of teachers finding real, relevant, engaging lessons for their students at the #MakeItReal hashtag on Twitter, too. Here's another example from a middle school.

After telling my story about the Red Cube sculpture to a group of teachers in Minnesota, one seventh-grade teacher remembered that there is a giant sculpture in Minneapolis called Spoonbridge and Cherry. Here it is.

Image 3.1: Spoonbridge and Cherry, by sculptor Claes Oldenburg Coosje van Bruggen.

That teacher knew that her students saw this all the time, so she decided to build a lesson on scale factor around it.

She showed her students the picture and immediately they started sharing stories of how they'd seen it every time they went to their grandmother's house or how they went to that park last summer and it's a lot bigger than it seems from the road. These stories led to the exact questions she wanted to ask. Students then spent time comparing this spoon and cherry to a real spoon and cherry, estimating and scaling, as well as estimating and scaling the size of a person who'd hold this spoon and eat this cherry. It even went off to answering the question of whether the spoon and cherry were in the correct proportion with regard to each other.

This was a significantly more interesting lesson than her previous packet where students drew images on graph paper that were two or three times as big as an original image. This was connected to her students, so it was relevant to them. Now every time they drive by it, they can share details about Spoonbridge and Cherry, which I'm sure their parents love to hear ... every ... time.

Why is it important to make math relevant, engaging, and interesting to our students? The National Center for Education Statistics reports that a meager 0.8 percent of students who go to college major in mathematics, while an additional 3.5 percent major in engineering. That's less than 5 percent of our students who go into careers that will "use math in real life." How many students do you teach? Twenty? One hundred twenty? Then you've got between one and six of your students who might major in a high-level mathematics subject in college. Those are the students who are already interested in your course.

The other 95 percent need to see the beauty of mathematics, the existence of it in the world around them, and they need to learn to find mathematical questions worth thinking about and answering. They don't all need to be experts. We make math relevant, engaging, and interesting to our students because when they leave our school we want them to be problem solvers, mathematical treasure hunters, and to wonder about the math behind what they see.

SOLVE THE CALCULATOR CONUNDRUM

Choosing an instrument for all students: Desmos

Man is a tool-using animal. Nowhere do you find him without tools; without tools he is nothing, with tools he is all.
— THOMAS CARLYLE, SCOTTISH PHILOSOPHER

THE PROBLEM: STUDENTS DON'T KNOW HOW OR WHEN TO USE A CALCULATOR

IN A STRANGE turn of events, one of the staple comments that I was told by my math teachers and that I told my own students when teaching them at the beginning of my career has been completely reversed and is absolutely no longer true. What was this statement that I, and likely some of you, told our students? This: "You've got to know how to do this because you won't have a calculator with you wherever you go after you graduate." As life and advances in cellular telephone technology would have it, they do have a calculator with them everywhere they go. It probably even talks to them, so they don't even need to read an answer. If they've got the right apps installed, it may do math for them before they even ask it to.

Teachers are spending time teaching the tool instead of using the tool to teach.

The problems now are: When is it OK to use a calculator? What type do I need? And how should I use it? The answers to these questions vary, depending on the grade level you teach, the state or country in which you live, and your goals for the lesson. In many places, like in New Jersey where I live, students take the PARCC standardized assessment in math. Your state might offer the Smarter Balanced Assessment or its own standardized assessment. Each of those tests has different calculator requirements based on grade level and course. For example, on the PARCC test for grade six, students can use a four-function calculator. They can use a scientific calculator on the eighth-grade test and a graphing calculator on Algebra 1 and higher. On the third- through eleventh-grade English assessments, surprisingly enough, they are not allowed to use a calculator at all.

What I've found troubling is that many teachers do not include the calculator as an effective tool in class, but merely take it out to show the students how to turn it on, push its buttons in the right order and find important symbols or menus so that the students will know what to do with it on the test. The problem is that even though they may know what to do with it, they often don't know when it's appropriate to use it at all. Teachers are spending time teaching the tool instead of using the tool to teach. Let's look at the calculator conundrum together.

THE HACK: SOLVE THE CALCULATOR CONUNDRUM WITH DESMOS

You may still be struggling with knowing when to suggest a calculator in class. Here's a tool analogy for you. Have you ever pounded a nail into a piece of wood with your fist? Of course you haven't. That's what hammers are for. So if you know that you need to pound a nail into a piece of wood, and you know why you need to pound the nail into the piece of wood, and you want to make sure that the nail actually does get into the piece of wood, then you reach for a hammer.

Are you teaching your students how to solve quadratic equations or simplify radicals or add fractions? Are they losing points on your tests, not because they can't solve quadratic equations or simplify radicals or add fractions, but because they made a mistake on a previously taught arithmetic skill? Then they should be using a calculator. If, at any time, the learning of a new concept is impeded by our own need to make sure our students can do it all in their heads, then we are the ones making the mistake.

Which tool do you choose? If you looked into my toolbox in my garage you'd see drill bits, screwdriver bits, hex wrench bits, socket wrench bits, and other assorted bits. That's because I have one favorite tool in my toolbox: my power drill/driver. On its own, it doesn't do anything but spin. But when the right bit is installed, it can drill holes of all sizes, insert or remove screws of any type into any space, loosen or tighten even the most stubborn of nuts and bolts, and even power saw pumpkins into jack-o-lanterns (I speak from experience). In the hands of someone who knows what it's for, how to modify it, or even how to hack it for a new purpose, the tool becomes more than just a spinning device. It makes hard jobs easy, impossible jobs possible, and is right there when I'm not sure what to do next. It becomes a necessity. Do you want a tool that can do all of that in your classroom? It is Desmos.com.

Desmos is a four-function calculator, a scientific calculator, and a graphing calculator all in one. But it's much, much more than that. In fact, it's so much more than that that the Smarter Balanced Assessment has abandoned its ties with Texas Instruments and signed on Desmos as its embedded calculator for the online assessment. The real gem of Desmos is not that it's a three-in-one calculator solution, but that it includes an Activity Builder that turns the calculator into a tool for investigation, learning, teaching, student management, and deep mathematical understanding.

WHAT YOU CAN DO TOMORROW

Let's stop taking pride in our ability to draw a really great sine curve or to find a common denominator faster than our students can find it. Instead, let's take pride in our ability to create an activity that teaches our students that the tools are available for their use, but they've got to know when and how to use them. Here's how you can get started tomorrow so you will be prepared to introduce it to your students.

- **Go to desmos.com and start graphing.** Visit the website. Once there, check out the four-function and scientific calculators on the bottom of the main page. Then click the Start Graphing icon and play with the grapher a bit. You'll soon see how much more powerful it is than student handheld calculators.

- **Go to teacher.desmos.com.** This is the hub of the Desmos Activity Builder. The educators and developers at Desmos have created excellent activities for you to investigate as a teacher, try as a student, and copy for yourself so you can modify them to meet your students' needs. Take a look at what's already here.

- **Go to learn.desmos.com.** Ready to dive deeper into how to make cool things like moveable points, animated graph features, and your own activities? Head here to access instructions and tutorials.

- **Visit the activity bank.** Remember the MTBoS from Hack 3? Well they've put together a Desmos activity bank at mtbos. org/desmosbank. Search there for your grade level and content area and see what's out there already.

A BLUEPRINT FOR FULL IMPLEMENTATION

Step 1: Start by test-driving the tool yourself.

By investigating the calculators, grapher, and various styles of activities available through Desmos, you'll have a strong sense of what you can do to Desmos-ify your classroom. You may want to introduce Desmos to your classroom as a display tool and show students a concept visually. Take time to get to know the different functions of Desmos. Once you can effectively use the grapher, making activities will be an easy-to-learn experience. If you want to see great examples of what other teachers and students are doing with Desmos, go back to the main site page and scroll down. You'll see featured art made with the grapher and also staff picks of their most interesting mathematics examples created by users. Not only can you share these in your class, but you can learn how to make them yourself by checking out the math that was done to create them.

Step 2: Swap out an upcoming lesson for a Desmos activity.

You'd be surprised how much your students can learn without the information being told to them directly. Desmos activities encourage investigation and conversation and can often reveal that your students know much more about a topic than you previously thought they knew. If you've got a lesson on quadratic graphing coming up, teach the Match My Parabola activity instead. If you're teaching place value, teach the Place Value Polygraph, which is a game like the one you may have played as a kid, Guess Who. If you're teaching about linear functions, you can likely swap out the entire chapter and replace it with the Linear Bundle of activities that Desmos has prepared.

Keep in mind that the library of activities on the Desmos page is not exhaustive, but is instead a collection of activities created by the Desmos team and by users. If you want more, visit the MTBoS bank or just Google what you want with the phrase "Desmos activity." You'll find what other teachers are making. Go ahead, try searching "systems of linear equations Desmos activity" and see what you get. You will be surprised how easy it is to find what you need and swap out a lesson.

Step 3: Request observation and feedback.

If there's one thing that will build support for the Desmos calculator and activity builder in your school, it's just giving people the chance to see it. The phrase I hear most when teachers and administrators see it in action for the first time is, "I wish I'd been able to learn math this way." That's powerful. Once you're comfortable leading an activity in class, call in peers or administration for feedback on your new method of teaching a topic. Not only will this show transparency on your part about sharing a new tool, but will likely garner more support for moving ahead with Desmos among other teachers as well.

Step 4: There's a time and a place for the handhelds, too.

Most smartphones have the capability to be a calculator. In fact, in most cases, you can just ask your phone a math question verbally and it will answer it for you. My Android phone automatically starts reading me the answer out loud when I ask it a question. But it depends on the question I ask. Here's a conversation I had with my phone today:

> "OK Google. What was my average rate of speed if I drove 472 miles in six and a half hours?"
> "I do not recall."
> "OK Google. What is 472 divided by six and a half?"
> "472 divided by six and a half is approximately 72.6153846154."

The one message we've told our students about calculators that is still true is that they will only do what you tell them to do. In this case, the smartphone calculator didn't recognize the context of my first question as a calculation question, so instead it searched for a fact that it might have known. It never found that fact. This is often how our students act when confronted with a math question. Instead of looking deeply at the question, they search for a fact or a procedure to apply—often not finding it, or applying the incorrect one. It's our job to make sure they can tell what a question is asking and determine what needs to be done to answer that question.

If arithmetic calculation or graphing are necessary to solve the problem, then it's time for the tool to spring into action. Giving them a calculator at this point in the problem will give them numbers or visuals they can use while the problem is still fresh in their minds. If they have to take time to pull out a sheet of scratch paper and do a large multiplication problem or hand graph points to analyze, they've often lost the flow of their thoughts and come back with a confused "where was I" feeling.

OVERCOMING PUSHBACK

There will be a handful of people who still think that anything that can be done with a calculator should be taught to mastery before ever touching the device. They usually also think that knowing trig tables will help in case there's a nuclear apocalypse. Here's how to assuage their fears.

The kids aren't really learning the math if they're using a calculator. My daughter, who's in eighth grade, was simplifying rational expressions which contained negative exponents and constants on a test. In the problem, she changed every negative exponent to a positive exponent correctly and also simplified the variables afterward correctly. At the start of the problem, she made the mistake of reducing 8/12 to ¾ instead of ⅔. She lost two out of six points on the question for this. You tell me, does she deserve a D on this question because of an arithmetic mistake that could have been calculated with a machine? I don't think so. But now she thinks that she doesn't know how to simplify rational expressions with negative exponents. Luckily enough for her, she has a math teacher at home to tell her the opposite. Not every kid has that. For the teacher with this pushback problem, I ask: Are you really assessing the math they're learning or just their ability to do arithmetic again?

They can't use Desmos on standardized tests. This is rapidly changing. In fact, the Smarter Balanced Assessment, which is offered in fifteen states (PARCC is only in nine), signed a partnership with Desmos, which is now the embedded calculator on the assessment for all test takers in grades six to twelve. Desmos even partnered with the assessment to offer an accessible calculator for blind and visually impaired students. Add to this the fact that the calculator is free for teachers and students, and according to the founder, Eli Luberoff, always will be, and you've got a relative likelihood that Desmos will overtake Texas Instruments on the testing market soon.

If Desmos activities are so good, then what's the point of having me there? Show these teachers the teacher.

desmos.com teacher dashboard of an activity. There they can see that they're able to manage the pacing of student work, see every student's response to every question, see every graph each student made along the way, overlay them for investigation, pause the activity and ask questions or point out interesting developments, and much more. Desmos activities put the teacher into the place of the highest value, as analyzers of their students, individually and as a group, and as expert decision-makers on how to proceed with each student's learning.

THE HACK IN ACTION

In my own earlier classroom, I applied what I called the TicTac method. It stands for Teach, Investigate, Calculate... Talk, Act, Check. I would Teach a topic briefly then ask students to continue to Investigate it through materials I prepared (I wish I'd had Desmos during those years). Then they'd need to Calculate to have information to use, so at this point it was calculators out. Why would I stop the flow of thinking to have them hand calculate when what I needed them to do was obtain numbers to use in the next step, Talk? After they'd gotten their calculations, they'd talk about what they thought they meant in the scope of the problem, maybe even revise their work based on the conversation, and then Act on their conversation to continue solving the problem to the end.

The last step, Check, would also include the calculator. Why would I have them plug their answers back into a problem and hand calculate to see if they were correct, when they could find that out faster by using a calculator—and if it was incorrect, go back and make a strategy or procedure change? The TicTac method put the calculator in its place as a tool for helping the learning process. I never told them to take out their calculators so they could get used to where the buttons and features were for the standardized test coming up. That doesn't really inspire an understanding of when to use the tool.

I recently modeled a sixth-grade Desmos lesson for a middle school where I was doing professional development in New Jersey. The lesson was on comparing rational numbers and fractions, so I prepared an activity for students. These eleven-year-olds easily logged into Desmos, signed in with their Google accounts (a necessary step if they ever want to go back and finish an activity later), and began the activity. On one slide of the activity, they were dragging and dropping points on a number line to estimate where they thought $\frac{3}{5}$ might be. I noticed from the teacher dashboard that there were two distinct areas where students were placing the point, so I clicked the pause button on the activity. When I did this, every student's screen went gray and showed, "Activity paused."

With no words on my part at all, twenty-four sets of eyes looked right up at me as if to say, "Why did you stop us?" I now had their attention and was able to ask questions about their estimates, the two areas of prominence, and what they expected to happen in the next estimate. I released the pause and let them go back to the activity.

I never would have been able to see all twenty-four students' work like this if the activity was on paper. After walking around, I might have seen a trend, but Desmos allowed it to appear instantly and serve as an instructional tool while it was still happening. This is just one example of how a power calculator tool with multiple features can change the nature of your instruction for the better. You've got to know which bit to put into the drill, so start looking for it.

There is significant value in students knowing math facts and how to calculate in their heads. Our brains are the fastest calculators in the world. How else do you think we can shoot a basketball into a hoop from thirty feet away? A math teacher takes forty-five minutes to calculate this with students; a basketball player solves the problem before knowing it's a problem. But in the system in which our students are schooled, they learn new concepts every day and sometimes before they're ready. If you find that your students' grades, or more important, their actual conceptual understanding of a new topic, are being held back by a struggle to get the basic math component of a problem correct, then give them the hammer and watch them build. And when you're ready, make Desmos a part of your class every day.

ASK UNANSWERABLE QUESTIONS

Engaging students in statistical thinking instead of skipping that section

Be able to analyze statistics, which can be used to support or undercut almost any argument.
— Marilyn vos Savant, American Author, Columnist, and Genius

THE PROBLEM: STATISTICS FILL DAILY LIFE, BUT NOT MATH CLASSROOMS

YOU'VE JUST ABOUT finished a chapter in your textbook or unit in your curriculum materials and then you notice it, right there, staring you in the face. What is it you see, menacingly staring back at you? The last section of the chapter: the statistics section, sometimes called "statistical connections" or "data around us" or "modeling." No matter what it's called, it gets translated by a lot of math teachers as "Skip me, you don't have time." But don't jump on the skipping bandwagon.

Find the mean. Find the median. Find the mode. Make a bar graph or pie graph. What's the probability of flipping heads on a coin? Twice? These are the instructions and questions that encompass the complete statistical learning many of us received in middle school, mostly with data sets of five to ten pieces of information. Some of us who had more adventurous teachers may have even made graphs of bivariate data and tried to come up with our own lines of best fit using completely non-statistical methods by employing our understanding of writing a linear equation using two points.

We live in a different world now, where large data sets are available instantly and calculation tools can organize and calculate all we need to know in less time than it takes to sharpen our pencils. It is no longer useful to spend our time teaching arithmetic and calling it statistics. In today's classroom, the mathematics teacher has the opportunity and responsibility to create statistical thinkers.

Unanswerable Questions will develop statistical thinkers in your classroom.

Rather than dwell on the past, let's look at the present and the future for most of us. Our standards and materials spell out the statistical concepts we are to teach. What has changed for our students is that the standards no longer ask for students to calculate and find statistical values, but instead to recognize relationships, understand variability and its effect, and make predictions based on interpretation of data. In short, true statistical thinking is missing. Statistics in today's schools should be based on Unanswerable Questions.

THE HACK: ASK UNANSWERABLE QUESTIONS

When we ask students to find the mean of the heights of the twenty-three students in our class, we are asking them to average numbers together, which is a very easy question to answer and an even easier question to grade. Instead, when we ask, "How tall is the seventh grade?" our students must begin an investigation that takes them much deeper into statistics. They will discuss how to obtain the necessary information, devise a plan (one that likely won't work or is completely unrealistic), refine that plan, measure each other, standardize their measurements, find means, graph information, and maybe even come across the idea of a distribution of data. That's all before the teacher even needs to get involved.

Since up to this point in their mathematical education, most questions have had numerical and final answers, the desire to answer an unanswerable question will continue to motivate the students to work and think and collaborate. Finally, they will come to a point where they are satisfied with their inexact solution to the problem, therein revealing the heart of statistics: using what we know to infer about what we don't know until more information comes along and either changes our minds or gives us a reason to reopen the question. Unanswerable Questions will develop statistical thinkers in your classroom.

WHAT YOU CAN DO TOMORROW

There's a reason your textbook or curriculum source has the stats section where they do. It's very likely that it ties into the unit you're teaching in a deep, meaningful way. Here's how to start harnessing the meaning and inspiring your students to think statistically.

- **Look at the statistics section first.** See what statistical concepts are connected to the lessons you're teaching in this unit, and work backward. Find an Unanswerable Question that you can share as you open the chapter, and refer to the question throughout.

- **Find claims in the media to discuss.** Every single day, you can find stories in the media with claims made about a company, a government office, an auto manufacturer, or a school. Present students with the opportunity to debate those claims. It's likely that in little time, they'll need a statistical process to back up their claims.

- **Share the unlikely.** Lottery winners, survivor stories, and game show outcomes will foster a statistical conversation in a hurry. When you read about them or see statistics in the news, make note of it and bring it to class to start those conversations.

- **Find Unanswerable Questions in sports.** Don't ask answerable questions, like what a player's batting average is now that he's struck out three times in a row. Dig deeper for the Unanswerable Question, like asking if batting average affects salary in baseball. Or which baseball stat has the biggest impact on player salary? Those are tough, if not impossible to answer.

A BLUEPRINT FOR FULL IMPLEMENTATION

Step 1: Commit to teaching the statistics section.

There's no way around this. You can no longer skip the statistics component by using the excuse that it was pretty much already taught in the other sections. Instead, move it to the front of the chapter and begin with statistical exploration. If you look carefully at the statistical component of the unit you're teaching, you can see the individual concepts that students will discover. For example, a unit on linear equations likely ends with a section on finding a line of best fit. It's a great way to incorporate all of the pieces of a linear equations unit. There's finding slope, finding y-intercept, writing equations for lines from the information, and more. The problem is that after teaching all of that individually, most students don't want to do it all again but with a set of data. By moving the statistics section to the front of the chapter, you open the door to creating a need for understanding slope, y-intercept, and graphing a line from a set of points. When students investigate a set of data that they don't yet have the skill to analyze, you become a mystery solver by teaching them how to solve the mystery, one piece at a time.

Step 2: Create an Unanswerable Question to connect the unit.

If you've put Hack 6 into action, then you're getting better at mathematical prospecting for questions. Put that skill into action here and see what you can find in the statistics section. A challenge can be very effective. If you were to find a claim from a company, like "Diet Dr Pepper tastes more like the real Dr Pepper," that your students could grab onto and argue over in your class, you've got a launchpad for a great Unanswerable Question. Take the time to look at the statistics sections in each chapter or topic deeply enough so that when a great question that connects to the content appears, you'll know it.

Step 3: Be statistically relevant.

If it's the last week of January and you've got a unit that you've identified as one that is loaded with univariate data analysis and modeling, don't give your students data on serve speeds from professional tennis. That's a summer sport; not relevant. However, the Super Bowl is happening in about a week, and it's an open field of potential questions. Maybe you ask students to think about how to price tickets in this year's Super Bowl stadium. Maybe you have them analyze team data to predict winners or outcomes or make pretend bets on the game. They'll be a lot more interested in answering questions about that in late January or early February than they will be in tennis.

OVERCOMING PUSHBACK

You may get more logistical questions than pushback questions on this Hack. Here are two that may come up, and how to address them.

How will you grade an Unanswerable Question? That's easy. You don't. The point of an Unanswerable Question is to generate discussion and the need for more learning. The great part is that even after the unit is done, the question may not be answered. This teaches students to be satisfied with a solution until more information comes along, then they can reopen the question for further discovery.

We use Chromebooks and they don't include statistics software. That's easy, too, because this isn't AP Statistics or a college course. Google Sheets has an excellent statistics capability on its own and the Explore feature can visualize data in ways you didn't know were possible. You can also install the Statistics add-on for Sheets and get more functionality. And don't forget our good friend, Desmos. If you investigated any of the activity bundles from Hack 7, you know that there are great statistics-based activities out there to foster engagement. Don't focus on the endpoint of statistical learning, which is the result. Focus on the beginning, which is investigation and statistical thinking.

THE HACK IN ACTION

One of my favorite Unanswerable Questions comes from a TV commercial that aired during my childhood. It involved a cow, a fox, a turtle, an owl, and a boy. The Unanswerable Question: How many licks does it take to get to the center of a Tootsie Pop?

Show the old commercial to your class—it's on YouTube. Then, after fending off questions like, "Why does the owl eat the lollipop?" and "Is this some kind of fable?" and "Why isn't the boy wearing any pants?" you can get started.

The Answerable Questions:

What are the characteristics of a Tootsie Pop that we need to take into consideration?

What is a "lick" for the purpose of the experiment?

What needs to be measured, and how?

In sixth grade, students need to be able to recognize that a statistical question is one that anticipates variability in the data. While the class is discussing and defining the components of the Answerable Questions, they will see that variability exists, even in their definitions, and as such, will exist in their data. Even when they come to an agreement on definitions and procedures, they will quickly find that during the data gathering, different students are following the procedures differently. This leads them directly into the next question: What do we do with our data?

Students may have enough mathematical acumen at this point to be able to make good, if not entirely correct, suggestions as to what should be done with the data—so let them. In my experience, by the third or fourth suggestion, they come up with "Average it all together," or "List it from smallest to biggest," and even "Graph it." At this point, I may break the class into teams to complete each of the different valid suggestions and report back, or I may take one of the suggestions and run with it, depending on the focus of our previous and upcoming content instruction.

Sixth graders need to be able to describe the distribution of the data using its overall shape, center, and spread, and recognize that its center describes all the data at once, while the spread (variation) describes how all the data is different from each other. They also need to be able to display the data on a number line (dotplot or histogram) and describe the distribution in context.

I expect my sixth graders to be able to say: "After licking both sides of our own Tootsie Pops until each student reached the chocolate center, we counted the number of licks per student on each side. The mean number of licks was ##. This was more/less than I expected. When we graphed the data, the distribution was almost symmetrical except for one point which took many more licks to get to the center. The median, or middle value, was less than the mean, and I think that's because of the large number of licks it took on one Tootsie Pop. No one licked more than ## times or less than ## times before reaching the center."

Remember, the goal with sixth grade is not to pass the AP Stats test, but to introduce data-gathering methods, require correct statistical language, and to develop the ability to describe sets of data. To extend this to higher grades, weigh the lollipops first and compare weight and number of licks as a linear relationship. (There's a surprise ending to that one that I won't divulge). Students should also discuss whether or not the Tootsie Pops could be called a "random sample," and what randomness is and why it is important.

Our students are motivated to be right, and eager to prove others wrong. A few have even come to me to learn the basics of confidence intervals and hypothesis testing because of their drive to answer the Unanswerable Questions. Build statistical thinkers. They will, in turn, question everything, fostering their search for answers, and providing a need for statistical education. Only then will they find value in the processes and procedures of statistical analysis. The study of statistics and probability has always been interesting to students, but we now have a unique opportunity to lead them to the realization that this study is more than interesting, it is necessary.

CREATE A WONDERWALL

Building a culture of inquiry

I'm sorry, but all questions must be submitted in writing.
— WILLY WONKA, IMAGINARY CHOCOLATIER

THE PROBLEM: THERE'S TOO MUCH FOCUS ON ANSWERS

IF YOU HAVEN'T noticed by now, I'm a big fan of good questions. If you truly haven't noticed, then you're probably not actually reading this book. Up to this point, a lot of my discussion on questions has revolved around teachers being able to find and ask excellent questions of their students. That puts our students in charge of answering those questions. But this should not always be the case. We have to value the questions *our students* ask in order to truly create a classroom culture where they are interested in answering the questions that *we* ask.

I taught high school math for thirteen years before becoming an administrator. Since then, I've observed teachers at the high school, middle school, elementary, and pre-K levels. If there is one common thread among students in each of those classrooms, it is that they are insatiable when it comes to asking questions. It's unfortunate though, that as students age, their questions deviate from a source of natural inquisitive interest and begin to focus more on procedures and "getting help." We can reinvigorate our students' passion for inquiry at any age by allowing their questions to come out at the moment they have them. The problem is, that's too many questions for you to answer if you still want to be able to complete any amount of curriculum during your one hundred and eighty days together.

THE HACK: CREATE A WONDERWALL

"By now, you should've somehow realized what you gotta do ... And after all ... make a Wonderwall." OK, I'm done with the Oasis lyrics now. What's a Wonderwall in the context of a classroom? It is a space on the wall where students can put up notes with questions they have. It may be about your content, but it may not. They may have said, "I wonder why pineapples look the way they do." Put it up on the Wonderwall. They may write, "I wonder how the company knows my water bottle holds twenty ounces" or, "How come I don't like broccoli?" or, "I wonder what my voice looks like." Yup, you guessed it: Put it up on the Wonderwall.

These questions will lead to a road of deep mathematical discovery and potential content learning that is far outside or beyond your course. Other questions might never be answered. But, when you display all questions for all students, you create a culture that says it's OK to question everything. Even better, students begin to investigate other students' Wonderwall questions, which builds a mathematical community.

WHAT YOU CAN DO TOMORROW

Got one of those big rolls of paper at school? Got scissors and tape? Maybe a fancy border from the local teacher supply store? You're ready.

- **Build the wall.** This has nothing to do with politics or border security. Decide on how you'd like the wall to look, and build it. If you're comfortable taking suggestions, let the students build the wall themselves.

- **Start with student questions.** Despite your potential desire to put a few questions of your own on the wall to start it off, don't. Students always know when the questions are your questions and won't believe that they're from students in "your other class." Let it belong to them.

- **Give the Wonderwall time.** Unless you give students a chance to add to the wall and see what's already up there, it'll just become a decoration. Give students time with the Wonderwall.

- **Listen for spoken wonderings.** Students often speak their wonderings without even knowing it. Listen, then tell them to add their thoughts and questions to the Wonderwall.

- **Speak and model inquiry.** When you see a great question or wonder on the Wonderwall, nonchalantly mention it at some point. Maybe even sit and start looking it up yourself. Show what inquiry looks like and that interest drives action.

A BLUEPRINT FOR FULL IMPLEMENTATION

Step 1: Build the wall, physically or digitally.

I'd suggest finding a space that is easily accessible for your Wonderwall. If students can't get to it, they won't go to it. There are a lot of ways to do this. For example, you could take a side wall by the doorway and create a space on the bulletin board or whiteboard. (Do you still have a chalkboard? How hipster.) Students could put up sticky notes in that space. It's a minimalist approach but it works. You might decide to section off a part of the wall with a border and decorations to draw attention to it. That's a bit flashier. Maybe you have a vision for the wall that includes putting a giant paper tree on your wall and filling it with Wonderwall leaves. That could be a lot of fun for the students who, when a question is answered, put it in a pile at the base of the tree like it had fallen there.

Giving young students a chance to share what they wonder builds their internal culture of inquiry.

Still, you may struggle with this idea because you're thinking, "I'm in four different classrooms during the day, and never the same one for two classes in a row. This Hack isn't for me." Yes, it can be! Make a digital Wonderwall with Padlet or Google Classroom to collect student wonderings and move from there.

Step 2: Promote the Wonderwall.

This type of activity is an excellent idea to share with other teachers in math and other content areas. It's also great to share with the Twitter community and other social media sites where you participate as an educator. Nothing is better than putting your spin on an idea out there and seeing how other teachers are inspired by it to create their own spin on your spin. You'll come away with great ideas to add into your own Wonderwall experience. Also share with parents through the same social outlets and email. They'd love to see that their kids are given time to investigate what interests them, especially in math class.

Step 3: Refer to the Wonderwall every day.

Give attention to the Wonderwall every day, and it will grow with more wonders that you can use as hook questions and other components of your lessons. By incorporating student wonders into your lessons, your statistical questions, or your Think Now warmups, you validate student thinking, student voice, and the Wonderwall itself.

Step 4: Celebrate new wonders and closed wonders.

As students come up with new wonders, intentionally or by accident, celebrate them. You don't have to have balloons and confetti set up in a net on the ceiling to bring attention to new wonders. Here are two reasons: 1. It may have taken a lot for that student to share an idea, so he or she should know that the effort, and in some cases, bravery, is valued. And 2. If you want students to become interested in the wonders on the Wonderwall, their interest will renew each time they hear the announcement of a new wonder. This may also remind them to bring up a question or idea they'd forgotten about.

OVERCOMING PUSHBACK

This Hack seems to beg questions from teachers and administrators. The following suggested responses are straightforward, and I've found them to be readily accepted.

Not all students will be interested in sharing. That's OK. There's a cycle of peer pressure with the Wonderwall that is interesting to watch. It may begin with peer pressure to not put up anything on the wall for social reasons, especially at the high school level. But after a few good wonders get up on the wall and you show genuine interest in investigating genuinely interesting questions, that social peer pressure breaks down and starts to shift in the other direction. Now the peer pressure cycle has moved so it is socially unacceptable to NOT put a wonder on the wall. Manage this well so students feel comfortable sharing. Remember, this is what they, as individuals, want to learn more about. That's important to value.

I share my classroom with another teacher. If you share with one other teacher, this just became Team Wonderwall. Both classes can put wonders on the wall, perhaps with different colors for different classes, or by mixing them all together. This just means that each student who shares a wonder will now have twice as many students who can help answer it. If the other teacher doesn't seem to be on board, just keep doing it for your own students. I have a feeling the other teacher will come around soon enough.

What if students put up inappropriate wonders? This is *Hacking Mathematics*; you'll want to check out another book in this series, *Hacking Classroom Management*. No system you put in place in your classroom should be a totally hands-off process for the teacher. Manage the Wonderwall and deal with inappropriate wonders, unless it's a really fun wonder such as asking a person to prom. Then I'm totally all for it.

THE HACK IN ACTION

The Wonderwall can take on many forms in the mathematics classroom. Jenna Cowell (@jenna_cowell) from the Greater Essex County District in Ontario, Canada, has created a Math Wonderwall with her elementary students. She puts up a question, an array, or an image for them to share their wonders about. Since they are young, this Wonderwall is part of a guided lesson where she scribes their wonders on the Wonderwall, which in this case is a large poster paper or whiteboard. Students can then explain their thinking or respond to another student's wonder on the spot. Giving young students a chance to share what they wonder builds their internal culture of inquiry.

Cheyenne Mills (@MsMillsKY) has built a permanent Math Wonderwall in a visible space in her classroom. She added two large sheets of poster paper over a background. On one sheet she puts her own wonderings about their current unit. Questions like, "What is a pattern?" and "How do patterns help us solve problems?" and "Why is place value important?" are on her sheet. The students fill the sheet next to it with their own wonderings and, as expected, their wonderings are much more interesting (no offense, Cheyenne). Their sheet has questions like, "Did patterns get invented?" and "Do patterns appear in reading?" and "How many things can you use place value for?" and "Do you see math in sports?" We can learn a lot from our student wonderings. Not only can we learn what they're interested in figuring out, but we can learn how to ask them questions in ways they understand. The Wonderwall can help us speak their language.

Cody Kikuta (@CodyKikuta) created a Math Wonderwall on Padlet for teachers, and asked them to fill it with their wonderings around math. The posts foster discussions among teachers and helps to generate ideas for classroom questions as well. You can check out his Padlet at tinyurl.com/ckmathww.

One of my favorite quotes, which I also included in my book *Instant Relevance*, is by David Cooperrider, professor of social inquiry and pioneer in the area of Appreciative Inquiry. He says, "We live in the worlds our questions create." It's absolutely true. When you hear a sound late at night and say, "What was that?" you're in a new world which harbors mystery, fear, or apathy (I am NOT getting up to check on that). When something you need breaks and you ask, "What do I do now?" you shift immediately to finding a solution or fixing what was broken. When our students see an object or concept in your classroom that sparks an interest and they say, "I wonder what that's all about?" it's our responsibility to open that world that our students just created. Place their new worlds on your Wonderwall.

COMMUNICATE THE MESSAGE WITH TWO-BY-FOURS

Creating community and parent buy-in

The two words 'information' and 'communication' are often used interchangeably, but they signify quite different things. Information is giving out; communication is getting through.
— SYDNEY J. HARRIS, AMERICAN JOURNALIST AND AUTHOR

THE PROBLEM: THIS IS NOT YOUR FATHER'S MATH CLASS

MATH CLASS AND math education are very different now than they were when our students' parents were in school. Even the youngest parent, maybe a twenty-seven-year-old parent of a five-year-old kindergarten student, learned math in the 1990s. Older parents (like me, but not my wife, who, if she is reading this, is definitely NOT old) learned math in the '70s and '80s. I have the benefit of having been a part of the gradual and sometimes abrupt changes in math education over the past twenty years, so when my own children need help or are struggling to understand a concept, I know how the current system is built and can help them appropriately. Most other parents have only one frame of reference when it comes to math: the way they learned it.

The problem lies in that most math-teaching methods from the past are either no longer being used or are taught in a different sequence. Take long division, for example. When I learned long division in third grade, I was taught the division algorithm with simple numbers of one or two digits. As the years progressed, we applied the algorithm to more difficult problems with more digits, and then decimals. Now, long division isn't taught until sixth grade or late fifth grade. Why wait so long? The shift comes from the placement of teaching division from a conceptual point of view first.

We teach students that division isn't a set of steps but is actually dividing up a number into parts. They get to choose whatever parts they're comfortable with when introduced to the idea of "partial quotients." We then progress to helping them learn how to be more efficient and pick the largest, most effective partial quotients they can to complete the division problem. Once they've understood the concept from this point of view, we introduce the fact that division problems can be complicated enough, and that using partial quotients may not be the best way to do it, but instead there's this process called long division. Long division, like a calculator, is a tool for a job. It is NOT the concept. That's why we need to give students the tool after they understand when it should be used.

How many parents of your current students have any idea that what I just described is happening? Probably none of them. So when Johnny Fourth Grader is struggling a bit with homework he doesn't understand (see Hack 2), Mom and/or Dad jump in with "Hey, let me show you this cool thing called long division. It's how I learned and it'll make your homework easier." They've just cut off Johnny's conceptual understanding of division. They thought they were helping, but instead they were adding confusion. Poor Johnny. And his parents won't know unless you tell them.

THE HACK: COMMUNICATE THE MESSAGE WITH TWO-BY-FOURS

Do we want parents to become experts at teaching our content so that they can be effective helpers at home? No. Do we want parents to feel like it's their responsibility to relearn everything they once knew to help their child keep up in school? Also, no. Do we want parents to make stuff up based on bad information, decades-old learning, and a false sense of self-confidence? Most definitely, no. Do we want parents to feel connected to their child's learning? Yes.

This is kind of like building a relationship. When you meet someone new, you don't jump straight to "Will you marry me" or "Let's quit our jobs and go on a fifty-state road trip." That's reserved for a time when you're closer, know each other better, and have the bank account to support such craziness (both marriage and the road trip). There's a tactic for building relationships with students at the start of each school year, and throughout the year as well. It's called two-by-ten. The idea is that you take two minutes a day for ten consecutive school days to talk with your students about topics that are not remotely related to school. This is also a great way to build relationships with your colleagues. Imagine talking with another teacher during the school day about something besides work pressures, what you're doing this week, IEP meetings, or that crazy math supervisor who keeps making you try Desmos all the time. It would be great! In fact, don't wait for it; start a non-school-related conversation yourself.

Let's apply the similar two-by-four Hack to our students and their parents. Take two minutes each day for four days each week and talk about nothing BUT what's being taught in your classroom. It's fine to use whatever method you already love for recording your thoughts. Then, send that two minutes' worth of talk home to the parents. Most parents will listen to or read two minutes' worth of information from you every day, I guarantee it (this is not an actual guarantee). I have four children in school and would gladly sacrifice eight minutes if it meant that I could talk with my kids as they did their math work for the night without having to spend thirty minutes or more "figuring out" what they're doing.

WHAT YOU CAN DO TOMORROW

I chose four days for two reasons. The first is that there is usually a day each week where new information isn't necessary to send home. The second is that calling this Hack two-by-fours is catchier than calling it two-by-fives, so there's that. This can start right away if you are already using a communication tool that you love. If you're not, I'll introduce you to a few you may like.

- **Choose your method.** One-way communication can be successfully implemented through email, Remind, Google Classroom, YouTube, Google Drive sharing, Vimeo, and more. Two-way communication can come from Flipgrid, Seesaw, Recap, Google Classroom, Twitter, Facebook, Instagram, and more. Pick one and stick to it.

- **Commit the time.** It's going to take you a minute or two to effectively summarize the lesson into your message. It'll take two more to write or record it. It will take a minute or two more to send it. Find the four to six minutes in your day and they will save many more in the long run.

- **In the first message, send the whole message.** Tell parents what you're doing, what they can expect, and that you promise to keep it to two minutes or less every time. They'll appreciate the consistency and be more likely to listen to what you have to share.
- **Share good summaries from students.** If your students must summarize their learning or explain themselves for an exit ticket in class, they may effectively hit the message in their explanations. Share their words, or if you collect video or audio from them, offer that instead. The variety and authenticity will keep parents interested.

A BLUEPRINT FOR FULL IMPLEMENTATION

Step 1: Start with an interesting big-picture message.

We're teachers, and as such, we're planners. Sometimes we feel the need to make a string of announcements before an event, like telling our students on Monday that there will be a quiz on Friday. And then reminding them on Wednesday, and making sure it's on our calendar, and sending a Remind message to their phones or parents on Thursday to make sure they all know that there will be a quiz on Friday. That's really helpful, because now the students have all week to plan how to fake being sick on Friday, and even have time to set up the prerequisite stomach aches earlier in the week, even though there's a math quiz that they "really don't want to miss, Mom."

Kids want to be involved, and if you reward their excellent explanations and clear mathematical communication, they'll continue to give you their best.

Because of our tendency to plan this way, we may feel the need to send out an email to parents on a Friday, letting them know we're starting our two-by-four initiative on the following Monday. While there are those who may appreciate this, many will know that on Monday they'll be getting a message to delete, skip, or avoid. Catch them off guard by sending your first, big-picture message in your chosen message format, out of the blue. Like a great Think Now question or Wonderwall moment, your delivery can hook them in for the long haul.

Step 2: Keep your word.

In your first message, establish that these messages will be coming, that they will be two minutes or less, and that they will be helpful and valuable. The only way to do this is to keep your word to parents and send messages on time that are short enough and helpful enough to do the job. I've been a part of classrooms where teachers tried to recreate their whole lessons every day, recording them and uploading them either to YouTube or a website for parents and students. While that may seem helpful, it is a time drain on the teacher, and most parents have shared feedback that the lessons were just too long to be helpful.

Step 3: Get feedback from parents.

You won't know for sure if they're watching your videos, reading your emails, or listening to your recordings if you don't ask. Get feedback from parents via a Google Form, Poll Everywhere or Mentimeter survey, or another method you like. They will share with you the strengths and weaknesses of the messages you send home, and as a reflective practitioner, you can make adjustments without taking it personally.

Step 4: Enlist a small army.

Of course, by a small army, I mean your students. They may be interested and even eager to be the ones who get to make and send the messages home. On a daily basis, I have pods of students who rush up to me to ask if they can do the Pledge of Allegiance or read off the daily birthdays. Kids want to be involved, and if you reward their excellent explanations and clear mathematical communication, they'll continue to give you their best.

OVERCOMING PUSHBACK

Despite the fact that sharing is caring, and parents regularly ask for more information about their child's learning, you may still come across a bit of pushback to your new communication initiative. Here are ways to work with it.

Parents who say they never get the messages. Make sure your communication channel is working fine. If it is, you may need to troubleshoot the issue with parents individually. Make sure you have their correct email addresses or verify if they're looking for your messages in the right place. It may be that they're at the wrong website or that your messages go to their spam email box because they still use AOL and are waiting for the next CD to show up with the latest upgrade for Windows 95. Help them connect to the message the first time, and then hold them accountable for it.

It's not enough for some parents. This is a fun one to field when it comes in. Guess who has the rest of the information that they want or need? Their child. Return the request for more information or longer videos with a redirect to a conversation with their child. Give them good questions to ask (see Hack 4).

Obtain necessary permissions. If you plan to share student voices or videos on a publicly available site like Twitter or YouTube, make sure you have obtained the appropriate permissions in your district. Otherwise, you can get around this by creating a private YouTube channel or by using tools like Flipgrid and Recap, which are only available to invited members.

THE HACK IN ACTION

Curtis Slater, principal at Wyoming Elementary School in Wyoming, Minnesota, (I know ... there's a Wyoming in Minnesota now?) and his staff communicate with parents and the community on a daily basis through Twitter. They take short videos of students explaining their learning, participating in activities, and performing musically. They instituted the Merry Math Week last year and have continued the communication as a way to engage students in making connections between math and the holiday season.

In brief communications, students and teachers share a math concept, skill, or question to be answered. Parents see what students are learning and how they're making connections. Many of the parents comment on the videos and have asked to participate in Merry Math activities. One of the best outcomes is that when the teachers shared what was taught and learned in class in a concise and interesting video, parents grasped onto it as a springboard for conversations at home.

My two-by-four Hack is a new take on the communication methods we've seen in the past. Many have been sporadic based on opportunity, or teachers have reached out with resources when students are struggling or when parents request them. I'm looking forward to seeing how you put the two-by-four Hack into action in your classrooms and hope you'll share your successes and learning with me on Twitter and at the #HackingMath hashtag, too.

We cannot underestimate the power of letting parents know that we value them and their interest in helping their children learn mathematics. Sharing these brief two-by-four moments with them sends the message that we will give them just the right amount of help to keep them involved at home without requiring them to become expert teachers. Many parents have the fear that they're inadequate at mathematics and can't help their kids anymore. Take away the fear and you'll see relationships grow.

CONCLUSION
Putting the pieces together

I HOPE THAT AS you've read *Hacking Mathematics*, you've recognized that I did not want to write a book about math tricks you can use in the classroom. If I'd given you ways to find prime numbers faster in your head, factor polynomials the Babylonian way, or use the Japanese lattice method for multiplication, then this book would have been a waste of time. Good mathematics teaching involves giving the students time to think deeply, ask questions, revise their work, learn from their mistakes, and talk with each other about what they've learned.

There are no tricks or hacks that will fix math education and the expectations people have for math teachers in today's schools. I've given you my best and the best others have to offer to support your teaching in the ever-changing school atmosphere in which we live and work every day. Think Now, Desmos, Lagging Homework, the MTBoS, and the Wonderwall can all impact your teaching and the experience your students have while they're in your classroom every day. That's the message. When you walk into your classroom, are you ready to carry out a lesson plan, or are you ready to give your students a mathematical experience that will impact them for life?

Do you have ideas for more hacks? Are you implementing ideas in your classroom that have had a big impact on mathematical learning and could have been mentioned in the pages of this book? Please, in the name of all that is good, share what you've done and learned with the world. Blog about it, tweet about it using #HackingMath, reach out to me and others, and let's spread the message together. Mathematics can be hacked successfully without detracting from the excellent pedagogy needed to teach it and the dedication and effort needed to learn it. There will be teachers who think none of this is worth the paper it's printed on. To them, I cycle back to G.K. Chesterton, mentioned in the introduction, one more time.

"It isn't that they can't see the solution. It is that they can't see the problem."

Because you are reading this book, I believe that you, me, and math teachers like us can not only see the problem, but can work together to be a powerful part of the solution.

OTHER BOOKS IN THE
HACK LEARNING SERIES

HACKING EDUCATION
10 Quick Fixes For Every School

By Mark Barnes (@markbarnes19) & Jennifer Gonzalez (@cultofpedagogy)

In the bestselling *Hacking Education*, Mark Barnes and Jennifer Gonzalez employ decades of teaching experience and hundreds of discussions with education thought leaders to show you how to find and hone the quick fixes that every school and classroom need. Using a Hacker's mentality, they provide **one Aha moment after another** with 10 Quick Fixes For Every School—solutions to everyday problems and teaching methods that any teacher or administrator can implement immediately.

"Barnes and Gonzalez don't just solve problems; they turn teachers into hackers—a transformation that is right on time."

—Don Wettrick, Author of *Pure Genius*

MAKE WRITING
5 Teaching Strategies That Turn Writer's Workshop Into a Maker Space

By Angela Stockman (@angelastockman)

Everyone's favorite education blogger and writing coach, Angela Stockman, turns teaching strategies and practices upside down in the bestselling, *Make Writing*. She spills you out of your chair, shreds your lined paper, and launches you and your writer's workshop into the maker space! Stockman provides five right-now writing strategies that reinvent instruction and **inspire both young and adult writers** to express ideas with tools that have rarely, if ever, been considered. *Make Writing* is a fast-paced journey inside Stockman's Western New York Young Writer's Studio, alongside the students there who learn how to write and how to make, employing Stockman's unique teaching methods.

"Offering suggestions for using new materials in old ways, thoughtful questions, and specific tips for tinkering and finding new audiences, this refreshing book is inspiring and practical in equal measure."

—Amy Ludwig VanDerwater, Author and Teacher

HACKING ASSESSMENT
10 Ways to Go Gradeless in a Traditional Grades School

By Starr Sackstein (@mssackstein)

In the bestselling *Hacking Assessment,* award-winning teacher and world-renowned formative assessment expert Starr Sackstein unravels one of education's oldest mysteries: How to assess learning without grades—even in a school that uses numbers, letters, GPAs, and report cards. While many educators can only muse about the possibility of a world without grades, teachers like Sackstein are **reimagining education**. In this unique, eagerly anticipated book, Sackstein shows you exactly how to create a remarkable no-grades classroom like hers, a vibrant place where students grow, share, thrive, and become independent learners who never ask, "What's this worth?"

"The beauty of the book is that it is not an empty argument against grades—but rather filled with valuable alternatives that are practical and will help to refocus the classroom on what matters most."

—Adam Bellow, White House Presidential Innovation Fellow

HACKING THE COMMON CORE
10 Strategies for Amazing Learning in a Standardized World

By Michael Fisher (@fisher1000)

In *Hacking the Common Core,* longtime teacher and CCSS specialist Mike Fisher shows you how to bring fun back to learning, with 10 amazing hacks for teaching all Core subjects, while engaging students and making learning fun. Fisher's experience and insights help teachers and parents better understand close reading, balancing fiction and nonfiction, using projects with the Core, and much more. *Hacking the Common Core* provides **read-tonight-implement-tomorrow strategies** for teaching the standards in fun and engaging ways, improving teaching and learning for students, parents, and educators.

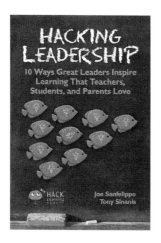

HACKING LEADERSHIP
10 Ways Great Leaders Inspire Learning
That Teachers, Students, and Parents Love

By Joe Sanfelippo (@joesanfelippoFC) and Tony Sinanis (@tonysinanis)

In the runaway bestseller *Hacking Leadership*, renowned school leaders Joe Sanfelippo and Tony Sinanis bring readers inside schools that few stakeholders have ever seen—places where students not only come first but have a unique voice in teaching and learning. Sanfelippo and Sinanis ignore the bureaucracy that stifles many leaders, focusing instead on building a culture of **engagement, transparency, and most important, fun**. *Hacking Leadership* has superintendents, principals, and teacher leaders around the world employing strategies they never before believed possible.

"The authors do a beautiful job of helping leaders focus inward, instead of outward. This is an essential read for leaders who are, or want to lead, learner-centered schools."

—George Couros, Author of *The Innovator's Mindset*

HACKING LITERACY
5 Ways To Turn Any Classroom Into a
Culture Of Readers

By Gerard Dawson (@gerarddawson3)

In *Hacking Literacy*, classroom teacher, author, and reading consultant Gerard Dawson reveals 5 simple ways any educator or parent can turn even the most reluctant reader into a thriving, enthusiastic lover of books. Dawson cuts through outdated pedagogy and standardization, turning reading theory into practice, sharing **valuable reading strategies**, and providing what *Hack Learning Series* readers have come to expect—actionable, do-it-tomorrow strategies that can be built into long-term solutions.

HACKING ENGAGEMENT
50 Tips & Tools to Engage Teachers and Learners Daily

By James Alan Sturtevant (@jamessturtevant)

Some students hate your class. Others are just bored. Many are too nice, or too afraid, to say anything about it. Don't let it bother you; it happens to the best of us. But now, it's **time to engage!** In *Hacking Engagement*, the seventh book in the *Hack Learning Series*, veteran high school teacher, author, and popular podcaster James Sturtevant provides 50—that's right five-oh—tips and tools that will engage even the most reluctant learners daily.

HACKING HOMEWORK
10 Strategies That Inspire Learning Outside the Classroom

By Starr Sackstein (@mssackstein) and Connie Hamilton (@conniehamilton)

Learning outside the classroom is being reimagined, and student engagement is better than ever. World-renowned author/educator Starr Sackstein has changed how teachers around the world look at traditional grades. Now she's teaming with veteran educator, curriculum director, and national presenter Connie Hamilton to bring you **10 powerful strategies** for teachers and parents that promise to inspire independent learning at home, without punishments or low grades.

"Starr Sackstein and Connie Hamilton have assembled a book full of great answers to the question, 'How can we make homework engaging and meaningful?'"

—Doug Fisher and Nancy Frey, Authors and Presenters

HACKING PROJECT BASED LEARNING
10 Easy Steps to PBL and Inquiry in the Classroom

By Ross Cooper (@rosscoops31) and Erin Murphy (@murphysmusings5)

As questions and mysteries around PBL and inquiry continue to swirl, experienced classroom teachers and school administrators Ross Cooper and Erin Murphy have written a book that will empower those intimidated by PBL to cry, "I can do this!" while at the same time providing added value for those who are already familiar with the process. *Hacking Project Based Learning* demystifies what PBL is all about with **10 hacks that construct a simple path** that educators and students can easily follow to achieve success.

"*Hacking Project Based Learning* is a classroom essential. Its ten simple 'hacks' will guide you through the process of setting up a learning environment in which students will thrive from start to finish."

—Daniel H. Pink, *New York Times* Bestselling Author of *DRIVE*

HACK LEARNING ANTHOLOGY
Innovative Solutions for Teachers and Leaders

Edited by Mark Barnes (@markbarnes19)

Anthology brings you the most innovative education Hacks from the first nine books in the *Hack Learning Series*. Written by twelve award-winning classroom teachers, principals, superintendents, college instructors, and international presenters, *Anthology* is every educator's new problem-solving handbook. It is both a preview of nine other books and a **full-fledged, feature-length blueprint** for solving your biggest school and classroom problems.

HACKING GOOGLE FOR EDUCATION
99 Ways to Leverage Google Tools in Classrooms, Schools, and Districts

By Brad Currie (@bradmcurrie), Billy Krakower (@wkrakower), and Scott Rocco (@ScottRRocco)

If you could do more with Google than search, what would it be? Would you use Google Hangouts to connect students to cultures around the world? Would you finally achieve a paperless workflow with Classroom? Would you inform and engage stakeholders district-wide through Blogger? Now, you can say Yes to all of these, because Currie, Krakower, and Rocco remove the limits in Hacking Google for Education, giving you **99 Hacks in 33 chapters**, covering Google in a unique way that benefits all stakeholders.

"Connected educators have long sought a comprehensive resource for implementing blended learning with G Suite. *Hacking Google for Education* superbly delivers with a plethora of classroom-ready solutions and linked exemplars."

—Dr. Robert R. Zywicki, Superintendent of Weehawken Township School District

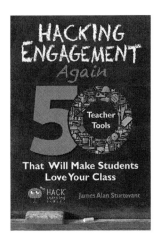

HACKING ENGAGEMENT AGAIN
50 Teacher Tools That Will Make Students
Love Your Class

By James Alan Sturtevant (@jamessturtevant)

50 Student Engagement Hacks just weren't enough. 33-year veteran classroom teacher, James Alan Sturtevant, wowed teachers with the original Hacking Engagement, which contained 50 Tips and Tools to Engage Teachers and Learners Daily. Those educators and students got better, but they craved more. So, longtime educator and wildly popular student engager Sturtevant is *Hacking Engagement Again*!

"This book is packed with ideas that can be implemented right away: Some creatively weave technology into instruction, others are just plain creative, and all of them are smart. Plus, the QR codes take the reader to so many more fantastic resources. With this book in hand, every teacher will find ways to freshen up their teaching and make it fun again!"

—Jennifer Gonzalez, Bestselling Author, Speaker, and CEO at CultOfPedagogy.com

HACKING DIGITAL LEARNING STRATEGIES
10 Ways to Launch EdTech Missions in Your Classroom

By Shelly Sanchez Terrell (@ShellTerrell)

In *Hacking Digital Learning Strategies*, international EdTech presenter and NAPW Woman of the Year Shelly Sanchez Terrell demonstrates the power of EdTech Missions—lessons and projects that inspire learners to use web tools and social media to innovate, research, collaborate, problem-solve, campaign, crowd fund, crowdsource, and publish. The 10 Missions in *Hacking DLS* are more than enough to transform how teachers integrate technology, but there's also much more here. Included in the book is a **38-page Mission Toolkit**, complete with reproducible mission cards, badges, polls, and other handouts that you can copy and distribute to students immediately.

"The secret to Shelly's success as an education collaborator on a global scale is that she shares information most revered by all educators, information that is original, relevant, vetted, and proven, combining technology with proven education methodology in the classroom. This book provides relevance to a 21st century educator."

—Thomas Whitby, Author, Podcaster, Blogger, Consultant, Co-founder of #Edchat

HACKING PARENTHOOD
10 Mantras You Can Use Daily to Reduce the Stress of Parenting

By Kimberley Moran (@kimberleygmoran)

You throw out consequences willy nilly. You're tired of solutions that are all or nothing. You're frustrated with the daily chaos. Enter mantras, invaluable parenting anchors wrapped in tidy packages. These will become your go-to tools to calm your mind, focus your parenting, and concentrate on what you want for your kids. Kimberley Moran is a parent and a teacher who works tirelessly to find best practices for simplifying parenting and maximizing parent-child communication. Using **10 Parent Mantras as cues to stop time and reset**, Moran shares concrete ways to parent with intention and purpose, without losing your cool.

HACKING CLASSROOM MANAGEMENT
10 Ideas To Help You Become the Type of
Teacher They Make Movies About

By Mike Roberts (@baldroberts)

Utah English Teacher of the Year and sought-after speaker Mike Roberts brings you 10 quick and easy classroom management hacks that will make your classroom the place to be for all your students. He shows you how to create an amazing learning environment that actually makes discipline, rules and consequences obsolete, no matter if you're a new teacher or a 30-year veteran teacher.

"Mike writes from experience; he's learned, sometimes the hard way, what works and what doesn't, and he shares those lessons in this fine little book. The book is loaded with specific, easy-to-apply suggestions that will help any teacher create and maintain a classroom where students treat one another with respect, and where they learn."

—Chris Crowe, English Professor at BYU, Past President of ALAN, author of Death Coming Up the Hill, Getting Away with Murder: The True Story of the Emmett Till Case; Mississippi Trial, 1955; and many other YA books

HACKING THE WRITING WORKSHOP
Redesign with Making in Mind

By Angela Stockman (@AngelaStockman)

Agility matters. This is what Angela Stockman learned when she left the classroom over a decade ago to begin supporting young writers and their teachers in schools. What she learned transformed her practice and led to the publication of her primer on this topic: *Make Writing: 5 Teaching Strategies that Turn Writer's Workshop Into a Maker Space*. Now, Angela is back with more stories from the road and plenty of new thinking to share.

"Good writing is good thinking. This is a book about how to think better, for yourself and with others."

—Dave Gray, Founder of XPLANE, and Author of *The Connected Company*, *Gamestorming*, and *Liminal Thinking*

HACK LEARNING RESOURCES

All Things Hack Learning:
hacklearning.org

The Entire *Hack Learning Series* on Amazon:
hacklearningbooks.com

The Hack Learning Podcast, hosted by Mark Barnes:
hacklearningpodcast.com

Hack Learning on Twitter
@HackMyLearning
#HackLearning
#HackingLeadership
#HackingLiteracy
#HackingEngagement
#HackingHomework
#HackingPBL
#MakeWriting
#HackGoogleEdu
#EdTechMissions
#ParentMantras
#MovieTeacher
#HackingMath

Hack Learning on Facebook:
facebook.com/hacklearningseries

Hack Learning on Instagram:
hackmylearning

The Hack Learning Academy:
hacklearningacademy.com

ABOUT THE AUTHOR

 **Denis Sheeran** is an engaging, fun, highly requested nationwide speaker, and delivers keynotes, full day workshops, and small group professional development to teachers and administrators. He is a Google Certified Educator, Chromebook in the Classroom trainer, Smartboard and Smart Notebook trainer, and can customize PD for your school district. Denis has a Masters Degree in Educational Leadership and a Bachelor's Degree in Mathematics Education with a minor in Music, and is an adjunct Professor of Statistics at the County College of Morris in Randolph, NJ. Before becoming the Director of Student Achievement for the Weehawken Township School District in Weehawken, NJ, Denis taught high school math, from Algebra to Advanced Placement, for thirteen years at Lake Forest High School in Lake Forest, Illinois and supervised the mathematics programs in Sparta, Edison, and Chatham NJ.

Denis lives in NJ with his wife, four children, and his litter box-trained dog, Scout.

Twitter: @MathDenisNJ
Blog: www.denissheeran.com

PUBLICATIONS

Times 10 is helping all education stakeholders improve every aspect of teaching and learning. We are committed to solving big problems with simple ideas. We bring you content from experts, shared through multiple channels, including books, podcasts, and an array of social networks. Our mantra is simple: Read it today; fix it tomorrow. Stay in touch with us at HackLearning.org, at #HackLearning on Twitter, and on the Hack Learning Facebook group.

Made in the USA
Middletown, DE
23 September 2018